THE

LEADERSHIP

EQUATION

LEADERSHIP, MANAGEMENT, AND THE MYERS-BRIGGS

BALANCING STYLE = LEADERSHIP ENHANCEMENT

By Lee and Norma Barr, Ph.D.

EAKIN PRESS ★ AUSTIN, TEXAS

A Word to the Reader

Change challenges people to grow and adapt — or get swept aside as obsolete in approach or technique. America has made astonishing breakthroughs in technology, but our understanding of people has not kept pace in the workplace.

The ultimate measure of leadership is the effect on people. *The Leadership Equation* addresses the foundation of leadership: people skills.

This book is written for people who are looking for a manageable, systematic foundation for building the people skills that leadership requires. Leaders must understand people. Leaders must also know themselves thoroughly and be able to accurately assess their impact on others. The Myers-Briggs Type Indicator is one of the most useful ways of organizing what you know about yourself and others. People who have identified their type through the Myers-Briggs will find this book most useful.

The guiding premise of our work is that a balanced individual style will produce leadership enhancement. People have natural preferences that affect the way they see, decide, interact, and control. These natural preferences will distort perception in leaders if they have not developed balancing skills.

Leaders should demonstrate and be able to help others develop people skills, such as

listening to the whole message instead of selectively hearing what you expect to hear;

perceiving accurately instead of selectively seeing what you want to see;

reading people's motives as well as their messages;

assessing people's potential accurately and knowing how to turn potential into action;

facilitating people of different style to work together cooperatively;

matching the right people to the right jobs and work groups;

and seeing your own strengths and weaknesses clearly.

Balancing style does not guarantee leadership, but it does provide the foundation for leadership enhancement.

Contents

Preface

A leader must do continuous, brutal self-examination to maintain clarity and balance. Power has a strong tendency to distort perception. Success also makes self-examination difficult.

In studying the lives of leaders, you can identify points in their lives when they tended to lose the ability to see realistically. The leader leads toward the vision and must keep it clearly focused, while seeing the facts as they are.

Hitler's vision of a powerful Germany made up of superior people was easily sold to economically depressed and frightened people. At what point did his vision become distorted by power and success, eventually rendering him incapable of reading the facts of the war? Look at the potency of his vision which caused rational people to doubt their own perception and to patently endorse Hitler's perception.

General George Patton's vision of leadership and war brought success against impossible odds. At what point did his intuitive insight get derailed by his lack of attention to the facts of politics?

When you think about a leader who lost the ability to lead, the question of balance arises. How does a leader maintain clarity to see what is needed at each turn in the road? When does the pattern of solving today's problems by yesterday's methods result in failure?

As a person becomes recognized as a leader, the opportunity to get clear feedback is considerably diminished. No matter how personable the leader, we are deeply programmed by stories of the king beheading the bearer of bad news. The more power the king has, the more people are careful about what they tell him. Similarly, the more you become recognized as a person with power, the more difficult it is for you to get objective information.

To be an enduring leader you must be clear about your strengths and weaknesses. You must know your tendencies to filter information, your preferences in decisions, and your personal idiosyncrasies. Remember: they don't seem like idiosyncrasies to you. The leader can be sure that the clever enemy has studied the leader thoroughly and has developed strategies to attack leader weaknesses and avoid leader strengths.

The Myers-Briggs Type Indicator is a useful instrument in helping to get a clear description of your natural tendencies. It is a non-normative instrument of 126 questions. Answering the questions quickly and honestly will reveal preferences along four dimensions: (1) extroversion-introversion, (2) sensing-intuiting, (3) thinking-feeling, (4) judging or perceiving.

Katharine C. Briggs and her daughter Isabel were a team of researchers deeply interested in human behavior. That interest resulted in the Myers-Briggs Type Indicator. In 1962 Isabel Briggs Myers published a manual for the indicator. In establishing the validity and reliability of the instrument, she made it useful to professionals. Since that time the Myers-Briggs has been used by more and more people, particularly the private sector. Its effectiveness has been realized by managers who continually need to more accurately read people and match people. The descriptive instrument yields invaluable information for individuals, organizations, couples, friends, and professionals.

Barr and Barr Consultants has administered the instrument to several thousand managers and executives. We continue to find it one of the most useful methods of enabling people to get a clear picture of their preferences. Participants can answer the questions, determine their scores, and receive a clear description of their style. They can then evaluate their description by checking experience and patterns that confirm or deny the credibility of the information.

One young manager filled out the Myers-Briggs, handed it over, and said, "I've taken a lot of these little questionnaires and I don't find them to be useful in the real world, but I figured what the heck. I gave it my best shot and I'm willing to see what you do with it."

Then as we began to work with the implications of preferences identified by the indicator, he frankly stated his surprise at the accuracy with which his feedback sheets described him. The pay-off came from his remarks, "This is incredible. This is like looking into a mirror and seeing the way other people see me. I've heard some of these things before and just wrote them off. Maybe there is something missing in my people skills, but before, I didn't even know where to start. This information offers a way to look at the process of the way I deal with people."

The Myers-Briggs Type Indicator is a useful method for helping a person do on-going self-examination. Isabel Briggs Myers said, "The gist of the theory is that much apparently random variation in human behavior is actually quite orderly and consistent, being due to certain basic differences in the way people prefer to use perception and judgment."

Perception and judgment are further explained:

"Perception" is here understood to include the processes of becoming aware of things or people or occurrences or ideas. "Judgment" is understood to include the processes of coming-to-conclusions about what has been perceived. If people differ systematically in what they perceive and the conclusions they come to, they may as a result show corresponding differences in their reactions, in their interests, values, needs and motivations, in what they do best and in what they like best to do. (p. 1, *Myers-Briggs Type Indicator Manual*)

A person's clear understanding of his/her own preferences enables clear, progressive development of the opposite preference. A leader must be able to extrovert and introvert, sense and intuit, think and feel, judge and perceive. If any of these preferences dominate too much, the leader's perception and judgment are affected. Skewed perception can lead to such distortion that failure results.

In the following pages we will describe preferences and styles of various people and the characteristics of those preferences. Personal experiences related in the book are written by Norma Barr; however, the book is entirely drawn from collaborative interplay of Lee and Norma's insights through work in their consulting firm.

From the eight categories of preference produced by the four dimensions, sixteen different types can be identified:

(E) Extroversion .... 0 .... Introversion (I)
(S) Sensing .... 0 .... Intuiting (N)*
(T) Thinking .... 0 .... Feeling (F)
(J) Judging .... 0 .... Perceiving (P)

* Intuiting is noted as (N) to distinguish it from Introversion (I).

Each person possesses all eight of the above. We are both introverted and extroverted, sensing and intuitive, thinking and feeling, judging and perceiving. Our style is composed of the preferences on each of those dimensions. We are usually more comfortable with one side than the other. Patterns of preferences are useful ways to identify leadership potential, adaptation to change, decision-making patterns, and interaction patterns.

The four dimensions and eight categories make sixteen possible types:

ESTJ	(extrovert, sensor, thinker, judge)
ESFJ	(extrovert, sensor, feeler, judge)
ENTJ	(extrovert, intuitor, thinker, judge)
ENFJ	(extrovert, intuitor, feeler, judge)
ESTP	(extrovert, sensor, thinker, perceiver)
ESFP	(extrovert, sensor, feeler, perceiver)
ENTP	(extrovert, intuitor, thinker, perceiver)
ENFP	(extrovert, intuitor, feeler, perceiver)
ISTJ	(introvert, sensor, thinker, judge)
ISFJ	(introvert, sensor, feeler, judge)
INTJ	(introvert, intuitor, thinker, judge)
INFJ	(introvert, intuitor, feeler, judge)
ISTP	(introvert, sensor, thinker, perceiver)
ISFP	(introvert, sensor, feeler, perceiver)
INTP	(introvert, intuitor, thinker, perceiver)
INFP	(introvert, intuitor, feeler, perceiver)

— 1 —

Personal Style, Management, And Leadership

Selecting the right person for the right job continues to be one of the serious challenges of management. Whether we like to admit it or not, matching the personality with the position is essential for success. I have heard managers argue that personality has nothing to do with their selections. They look only for producers. Yet, it is irrational to assume that a person's style is left in storage somewhere while performing managerial functions.

The title "director of finance" designates a position. The person filling that position determines what it becomes.

Personal style produces the impact of the position. Fill a service position with a power-oriented intimidator, and trouble begins quickly. Fill the position with a well-balanced person, and work processes begin to smooth out. People make the difference.

Companies and organizations need workers, managers, and leaders. The key element in all three is personal style. Some people seem to iritate without trying, while others facilitate naturally. The Myers-Briggs provides a useful structure for looking at personal style. It is a typology of human behavior that provides a skeleton for organizing all that you know about people.

Today's managers are taught formulas for management with a scattergun shot at problem-solving, decision-making, motivation,

1

conflict management, stress management, and communication. But what is the foundation for understanding people dynamics that makes all of those formulas understandable in the workplace?

The Myers-Briggs typology provides the needed foundation for reading and matching people. You can put two people together on one task and you may exponentially expand the trouble or the productivity. Is there a reasonably predictable way to sort human behavior? We believe there is.

Managers today desperately need to know more about people-management. That work begins with knowing oneself. In the eight categories of preference measured by the Myers-Briggs, a manager can get a clear picture of his or her own style and by comparison learn to see others more clearly. Managers should know about people. Leaders *must*.

Our work has convinced us that a leader must develop excellence in all eight categories to be able to lead consistently over time. "Flash-in-the-pan" leadership can occur occasionally, but development of long-term leadership capability requires self-development. Careful consideration of each of the Myers-Briggs dimensions will help identify tendencies and patterns of preferences that affect both management and leadership.

EXTROVERT-INTROVERT

These two terms are used the way Carl Jung originally explained them. Extroversion describes a process of primary focus on the external world of people and activities; introversion is more inwardly focused on ideas and concepts.

This one dimension sets the framework for the way we communicate. Extroverted managers tend to move around the organization more, engage in more casual conversation, feel comfortable tossing around ideas, and interact with more people. Introverted managers tend to concentrate more on work in their office, probe deeply into issues, deliberate carefully, and interact selectively.

My extroverted brother and I can go to the same party. On the way home he is full of talk about people and activities. He measures a successful party by his interaction with the largest number of interesting people and excellent dance partners. As an introvert, I am full of thoughts about the purpose of the party, the ideas discussed, and the concept of the event. I measure a successful party by whether or not I find stimulating conversation and an in-depth look at something that interests me. I like dancing too, but it is incidental to the conversation. Which one of us is right?

Preferences are not a matter of right or wrong; they are a matter of what feels most natural.

Extroverts like people, action, and activity. Introverts like privacy, introspection, and ideas. Managers who are primarily expressing their preference on this dimension affect their management positions by manifesting the same characteristics. Leaders, however, cannot sustain their roles over time if they indulge only in their preferred side of extroversion-introversion. Leadership requires balanced expression of both and accurate reading of people's actions.

Extroversion-introversion primarily determines our communication style. The next two dimensions of the Myers-Briggs are the communication channels for shaping our messages. The four communication channels involve ways of perceiving (sensing, intuiting) and ways of deciding about what we perceive (thinking, feeling).

SENSOR-INTUITOR

Our preference for sensory or intuitive information affects the way we see the world. People with a strong sensory preference prefer real world information that can be verified by their five senses. They are most comfortable focusing on the present and interpreting anything new by what they have already experienced or can validate with physical sensation. Their counterparts, the intuitors, interpret information according to its meaning, possibility, and implication. They, by nature, are not as focused on today. Possibility thrusts them toward the future. Sensors focus on what someone said. Intuitors focus on what they meant.

Sensors are good at spotting what is not working today and fixing it. Intuitors are good at spotting what is going to be a problem tomorrow and, therefore, plan around it.

Sensor logic takes ideas apart, while intuition puts things together.

Sensors prefer specific tasks with specific payoffs. Intuitors prefer complex problems with challenges in problem-solving.

Sensors develop step-by-step procedures for getting today's work accomplished. Intuitors reprioritize, refocus, and reposition for tomorrow's needs.

Managerial functions require both sensing and intuiting skills. Leadership cannot be maintained without excellent development of both ways of processing information. Sensing-intuiting are the channels through which we perceive.

THINKER-FEELER

The thinker-feeler dimension tells how we decide about what we see. We perceive through sensing-intuiting channels and we make decisions about our perceptions through thinker-feeler channels. This preferred way of judging affects our personal style. A feeler style handles managerial issues in a different way than the thinker style.

The thinker judges according to rationality of the information. A feeler judges according to the personal application of the information. The thinker values logical organization and the feeler values personal rapport with the information.

Thinker managers prefer objective approaches to their jobs, while feeler managers prefer personal relationships as a natural mechanism for doing their jobs.

A strong thinker preference may manifest in a cool, detached, uninvolved expression. A strong feeler preference may result in a warm, personalized, involved expression. The thinker appears to be head-dominated, while the feeler appears to be heart-dominated. In extreme expressions one seems like a harsh, critical person and the other seems like a weak bleeding heart.

Preferred use of the thinker or feeler channel affects our personal style.

Let's look at a conversation with four people, each with a dominant communication channel. They are working on a project.

Thinker: "You need to fire that guy." (Problem-solution)

Feeler: "He's got five kids and a sick wife." (Heart, people aspect)

Thinker: "That's not relevant. Your responsibility is to the company." (Logical frame of the problem)

Feeler: "My responsibility is to both." (Heart, people aspect)

Thinker: "It isn't reasonable to take on his personal problems." (Problem clarification)

Feeler: "You don't understand. He needs help. I can't stand to think what it would do to him. Surely there is something I can do!" (Heart, people aspect)

Sensor: "Let's get to work. We can't waste time trying to solve the world's problems. What's important now is our five-o'clock deadline to get this finished." (Task-focused)

Intuitor: "Even if we meet the five-o'clock deadline, the accounting department will sit on it another week anyway and then it has to go through legal, so our customer still won't get it as soon as he needs it. Let's try something else." (Implications and possibilities)

The way we see and decide affects our personal style.

JUDGE-PERCEIVER

The way we control is affected by our judging or perceiving preference. A strong judging preference indicates a desire to decide, evaluate, plan, organize, and maximize use of time. Judge-controllers have strong ideas about the way things should be done and the way people should be. Perceivers have a desire to adapt, respond, decide outcomes, and adjust as they go.

Judge-controllers want to get things finished and move on to the next challenge. Perceiver-adapters are interested in the process of doing and do not wait for a sense of closure to provide enjoyment.

Judge-controllers tend to work in a steady, orderly, planned way. Perceivers tend to work in a flexible, informal way. Judge-controllers drive toward closure, while perceivers like to discover tasks and manage emerging problems rather than plan for them.

Preference for judging or perceiving affects the communication channels. Judge preference tags the judgment channels of thinker or feeler as the dominant channel, while perceiver preference indicates that sensor or intuitor will be the dominant channel.

Our development as workers, managers, or ultimately as leaders is affected by our natural preferences of communication, information-processing, judging and controlling.

MANAGEMENT, LEADERSHIP, OR BOTH?

In turbulent times and radical change, leaders are desperately needed. The old manipulation-of-image strategy is not enough for the long term. Too often we have misused the word "leadership" to mean little more than clever control of image. In times of tremendous uncertainty, however, image is not enough.

Consider the way we describe the leader: *The leader is more fearless, more clear, more unlimited, more wise, and more courageous than anyone else around.* When social norms crumble and institutions go bankrupt and the war of perception is intense, people turn to the leader for stability. People turn to the leader to define reality and help them avoid the pain of chaos and insanity.

Change and uncertainty can be expected for the rest of this century. Outdated management techniques of planning around stable variables, stable markets, and stable work force are largely dysfunctional today.

Flexibility and clear thinking during crises are the critical characteristics for today's leaders. The image of leadership is no longer enough; the leader needs accurate perception in order to think clearly. S/he must also be willing to abandon old problem-solving methods that were dependent on identifying predictable variables that fit into rational equations. Today's rate of change requires a mix of fact and intuition, logic and feeling to top the crests of the unceasing waves of change. The leader must have the courage to explore the inner world in order to tap the resources required in uncertain times.

Consider the regulation-correct image of an ambitious young second lieutenant, leading a group of twelve into the unknowns of jungle combat. The lieutenant mastered the image of leadership with the spit and polish of uniform and the crisp physical control of movement and posture. He mastered the manuals and the theories. The real test comes with the first surprises, when all hell breaks loose and blood and blast disturb civilized reality and rehearsed war. What then? Leadership goes quickly to the one who thinks under fire, acts despite fear, sees what has to be done, and inspirationally activates the energy to do it.

The example reminds me of the status-correct corporate image of an ambitious young manager, thinking s/he is leading a group of twelve young professionals into the unknowns of corporate competition. As long as it is primarily an image game, s/he keeps control.

S/he emulates both a manager and a leader. But what happens in the face of devastating competition, reduction of staff, limited budget, and personal bank loans mysteriously called due? What then? Leadership goes to the one who takes charge, thinks on the feet, deals with the fear of financial ruin, and meets the situation with courage and wisdom.

Leaders frequently have to take the unpopular stand . . . to take the unprovable position . . . to lead people in a direction they don't want to go . . . to achieve something they are uncertain they can do. Those positions require strength and courage.

A leader must develop superiority in all eight categories of the Myers-Briggs to be able to lead consistently over time, not just in flash-in-the-pan situations. Let's focus on development for long-term leadership.

MANAGEMENT VS. LEADERSHIP

Management is commonly accepted as the process of getting work done through others by implementing major managerial functions. Courses in management teach the principles of these functions. They are commonly understood to be planning, organizing, implementing, coordinating, communicating, controlling, and evaluating. A review of each of the managerial functions follows.

Planning is divided into long- and short-range planning. Short-range planning is deciding what is to be done, where it is to be done, who is responsible for it, when it is to be done, and, at times, how it is to be done and which resources are involved. Long-range planning involves the overall direction the organization is taking, assessing future needs, developing resources to meet those needs, and acquiring or maintaining capital. Short-range planning relies heavily on sensor, thinker, feeler skills. Long-range planning relies heavily on intuitive, thinker skills.

Organizing is providing a structure to implement the plan. Aligning system components, establishing information linkages, prioritizing steps and procedures, establishing authority, and setting performance guidelines develops the structure. Organizing primarily uses sensing, thinking skills.

Implementing is issuing necessary authority, delegating tasks, and communicating instructions to get the plan going. Delegating authority, assigning jobs, consulting, guiding, and providing feedback is involved. Implementing relies on your communication ability, your sensing, feeling, thinking, and intuiting skills.

Communicating is the major managerial vehicle. It involves information and idea exchange, including verbal, nonverbal, written, and electronic information. Managers assign work, correct performance, negotiate differences, present ideas, and confront nonproductive behavior.

Controlling establishes work behaviors to insure that plans, goals, quality, and policies are achieved. It involves some way of knowing what is happening. Some system for collecting, analyzing, and evaluating pertinent information is needed.

Evaluating establishes norms for measuring results and determining acceptable variance from that norm. The manager takes corrective action when something isn't working well. Assessing quality, costs/benefits, productivity, and employee performance rounds out the function. All four communication channels of sensing, intuiting, thinking, and feeling are needed in evaluating.

Managerial *functions* are the categories of the manager's work. Managerial *skills* involve problem-solving, decision-making, communicating, perceiving, and judging. Managerial functions are inherent in the work; managerial skills are within the person.

Excellent attention to the managerial functions is no longer enough. Getting the job done in a cost-effective manner is important, but renewed emphasis on development of people is required for companies to maintain a competitive edge.

You may be arguing that management has always focused on people development. But consider this question: How many people get promoted because they are good at developing people? People usually have been promoted because they were technically excellent, they produced results, they were successful on a project, they knew the right people, or they had skills needed at the time. Rarely do you find a company or organization that continually selects its managers because they have the leadership capacity to inspire people. Ordinarily, selections are made according to technical expertise, seniority, priority, legality, or politicality.

Supervisors frequently are chosen because they were good at performing the tasks of their job. Managers frequently are chosen because they become politically astute about getting work through the system. Executives are frequently chosen because they have the connections and clout to deal with tougher, more complex challenges. Supervisors manage workers, managers manage supervisors, and executives manage managers. All three categories of management target different populations. Where do leaders fit?

LEADERSHIP IS THE PROCESS OF INFLUENCING PEOPLE TO GIVE THEIR ENERGIES, USE THEIR POTENTIAL, RELEASE THEIR DETERMINATION, AND GO BEYOND THEIR COMFORT ZONES TO ACCOMPLISH GOALS. LEADERSHIP IS A DYNAMIC PROCESS. IT AFFECTS, RISKS, DRIVES, INSPIRES, THREATENS, SUPPORTS, AND LEADS. LEADERSHIP DRAWS TRUST, AC-KNOWLEDGMENT, RISK, AND LOYALTY FROM THE LED.

Management affects work; leadership affects people. Management maintains orderly work systems; leadership maintains an enlivening, unfolding, dynamic development of people. They work well together, but they are not the same.

John is a manager. He is meticulous and orderly. The thirty people who work for him know what he expects. He plans and organizes the work and systematically implements the plan. As priorities change and problems arise, he carefully adjusts his plan. He systematically reviews employee paperwork, mathematically records their errors, patiently goes over work procedures as many times as it takes for them to get it right. After working for John, they will be trained technicians in the paperwork procedures of the company. He teaches and demands attention to detail in their work. But few people want to work for him. It's too boring and he's too tedious.

John's boss tried to develop John's leadership capacity, but the risk-taking capability was missing. John wanted to be an efficient manager, good at managerial functions. He did not see himself as a leader. He said, "I just don't want the personal vulnerability it takes to be a leader. I'm a plodder — not a pacesetter. Not everyone can be a leader. I'm content being a nuts and bolts man. I know I'm good at that."

Examine your own reaction to John's acceptance of himself. Are you judging him negatively because he is certain that he does not want to be a leader? He wants to be a manager. His unit produces steadily, if not innovatively.

Leadership requires you to maximize the style preferences you naturally prefer and to develop skills for your least preferred tendencies. John is an ISTJ (introvert, sensor, thinker, judge) and he is not interested in developing extroverted people presence, intuitive risk-taking, feeler sensitivity, or perceiver adapting. By choice he remains aloof, risk-adversive, detail-oriented, and tightly controlled. He does a good job of teaching procedural details. He plays a useful role in the organization.

In the current rush to develop leaders, traditional management education is being severely criticized. Bennis and Nanus, in their book *Leaders*, assert the following:

> "Management education" is, unfortunately, the appropriate description for that which goes on in most formal educational and training programs, both within and outside universities. Management education relies heavily, if not exclusively, on mechanistic, pseudorational "theories" of management and produces about 60,000 new MBAs each year. The gap between management education and the reality of leadership at the workplace is disturbing, to say the least. (p. 219)

Unfortunately, too many managers have attended prestigious business schools and come back more equipped than ever to intimidate people. Too often management is used synonymously with privilege. Agreement becomes more important than truth, style becomes more important than substance, conformity becomes more important than mission, damage control is more important than admission and problem-solving, mathematical skill becomes more important than people skill, and gamesmanship becomes more important than organizational health.

Paper has to be managed; people should be inspired. Work has to be managed; people should be motivated.

Leadership over the long term requires self-knowledge. You can learn managerial functions and develop managerial skills, but sustained leadership requires self-knowledge, self-realization, self-discipline, and self-development.

Let's look at a manager who wanted to be a leader. He was ambitious, intelligent, principled, and initiated into management.

CASE STUDY: NEED FOR BALANCE

PEOPLE: Joe Thompson — husband, father, and banker (thirty-two)

Ann Thompson — wife, mother, and college
graduate (thirty-one)
Tom Allen — Joe's boss (fifty-one)

ORGANIZATION:　Bank

Joe Thompson walked briskly toward his office, already imagining easing into his soft leather chair, swinging it away from the door, and facing the window. The panoramic view from his thirty-second floor window was Joe's favorite spot in the bank. He could relax a bit, let down his guard, and imagine flying into the lazy-looking clouds in his new Cessna.

Before Joe made it to the privacy of his own office, Tom Allen stopped him. "Hey, how's it going Joe? I just wanted to let you know — I've arranged a working lunch for you with the new owner of Woods Manufacturing. Great guy! You're going to like him. And don't forget happy hour with Wilson's guys. See you." Tom is senior vice-president of the second largest bank in the city, and Joe is Tom's favorite.

Tom identified Joe five years earlier as executive material and took over Joe's business life and some of his private time. Tom arranged contacts, assigned extra tasks, gave Joe complex assignments just to test him, and urged him to buy a house in the right neighborhood and attend a status church that afforded good business contacts.

As Tom walked away, Joe felt a tightening in his chest. He stepped up his pace and moved swiftly toward his office, but his secretary stopped him with an urgent message from his wife. He winced inwardly and thought about pretending he didn't get the message, but remembered Ann's thorough attention to detail. If he didn't call her back soon, she would call his secretary again, probing for details about his schedule and his delay in responding to her.

Joe went to his desk and reluctantly dialed the phone. Ann answered and described precise details of their two-year-old's 101-degree fever and the accompanying diarrhea. Joe fought to keep the irritation out of his voice as he recommended the medication the doctor had given them the last time. Ann detected a hint of irritation and immediately attacked him with accusations. "I'm sorry I bothered you with information about your son. After all, you have an important job dealing with people and their money. You don't care about me or the kids."

Joe withheld his own anger and attempted to soothe and reassure his wife. He reasoned that she needed his support and appreciation for the job she was doing. She eventually hung up after securing his promise that he would come home on time this evening so they could talk about their relationship. Too late, he remembered happy hour with Wilson's guys. He would just have to work that out.

Joe started to swing his chair toward his view, toward his release, when the buzzer sounded and his secretary's intense voice warned him that Bob Jones wanted to see him and seemed angry about something. Before Joe could replace the phone, Bob charged into his office red-faced and demanding.

"What the hell do you people think you're doing?" Bob raged. "My best customer expects top service and he's going to get it. Your out-to-lunch bunch is going to get off their tails and move that paper, or by god, I'll see that your department is sabotaged at every turn. You and Tom Allen think you can fancy-dance your way through this organization while the rest of us carry the load. Well, fella, you're wrong!"

Joe went numb inside and his thoughts seemed to belong to someone else. He seemed to be detached from them but vaguely heard a jumble of words — saw snatches of images moving in his head, heard bits and pieces of his own conversation: "Tom, you know this will make Bob Jones furious . . . a fighter, you know . . . of course I'll be home on time . . . I want to fly . . . get away . . . no . . . not now . . . I can't breathe . . . get that iron band off my chest . . . I . . ." Everything went black and Joe heard nothing more.

I first learned about Joe's heart attack from the president of the bank. He called and asked me if I could go to the hospital and talk to Joe and his wife. As a consultant I had worked with Joe in management development courses at the bank, so I was aware that he was a superstar being groomed for an executive vice-president position. He was already head of a department at twenty-eight and was learning fast. The past four years had been continual challenge and success.

The president said, "I don't know what the matter is with Joe. He had a heart attack last Wednesday. Bob Jones was in his office and Joe just slumped down in his chair and passed out. We've invested a lot of time and money in Joe. We've sent him to some of the most prestigious and costly banking schools in the country, and we don't want to lose him. See what's going on with him."

I realized that the president was looking at ecnomics. They had invested money in this young man and obviously wanted to protect their investment. So they would invest a little more and ask me to talk to Joe and Ann. Cover all bets. Get him the physicians to fix his body and a management consultant to try to fix his style. I was to see if I could determine the sources of tremendous pressure that had precipitated the heart attack.

As I drove toward the hospital, I thought about the pressures on today's executive. Success-oriented people tend to move into the competitive and narrow-space capsule of the quick-rise elevator to the top. They seem to accept the terms of the game without realistically assessing the costs. Joe had even talked to me about the game. His superior intelligence, superb academic background, and avid desire to learn had enabled him to identify the success game. He could talk about it in-depth. He intellectually understood it. Then, how could the pressure have gotten to him? It wasn't an unknown or unrealized factor. He knew about it. How did it get to him anyway?

The doctor briefed me on Joe's condition and remarked, "I've repaired the heart. Physically he can rebuild, but I don't know how to untangle the habits and patterns that got him in that condition. Maybe you can help identify the patterns."

I recalled interactions with Joe and remembered his communication style. He is a quiet, thoughtful, serious person — courteous and ambitious. How did all of this happen?

In the next two weeks I spent some time talking to Ann and Joe. Clues to their situation lay in the styles of the people principally involved. Basic preferences, habits of thinking and feeling, and ways of dealing with the world offered the insights.

Using the Myers-Briggs Type Indicator, we identified Ann's patterns. Joe's preferences had been identified earlier during management training. We looked at their habitual response to stimuli. Significant information is identified by the indicator about an individual's preference for privacy or interaction (extrovert-introvert), the preference for analytical or value-oriented decisions (thinker-feeler), the preference for practical or imaginative information (sensor-intuitor), and the tendency to control or adapt to situations and people (judge-perceiver).

The third person whose style was critical to this human puzzle was Tom Allen. Joe was quite different in style from both his wife and his boss. Joe's ambition and his values had teamed-up to diffuse his ego boundaries, and he no longer distinguished between his own preferences and the two people he had accepted as primary influencers in his life. Joe loved his wife and had made a conscious decision to be a good husband and father, as well as being a successful banker. Therefore, he began to accept the pressure from the evaluators of his success without mixing the evaluation with his own thoughts and feelings. He had tried to suppress his thoughts and feelings and act on the pressures.

Joe prided himself on his ability to set goals and stick to them. He had decided on the goals of good husband, father, and banker. That decision began to affect his perception. Every time he got that anxious feeling around Tom, he angrily reminded himself how lucky he was to be chosen. There were a lot of people in the bank who were envious. He argued vehemently against his own feelings.

That same tight control of feelings dominated his relationship with his wife. At his first realization of irritation with her, he would remind himself that she had postponed her career until their two children reached school age. He made excuses for her attempts to control his schedule. Although he really liked to spend time in his plane alone, she insisted that he not go flying without her. Joe ignored the way he really felt and tried to accept the requirements she laid down — since he had turned the full authority for determining whether or not he was a good husband and father over to Ann.

How could a bright guy like Joe get so fuzzy in his thinking? Let's look at some of the patterns that the Myers-Briggs Type Indicator showed.

Joe has a strong introvert preference, though you probably wouldn't detect that unless you are an astute people-reader. His social skills are smooth; he could be easily mistaken for an extrovert if you didn't pay careful attention to the way he uses his energy. On a bi-polar scale, Joe showed a strong preference score of 43 for introversion. He liked being alone, reading, imagining, or flying. His favorite flights were open skies without another plane in sight. Joe wrestled with the meanings of things and probed deeply into topics to discover the vertebra of truth. So, how did Joe become a fast-track banker?

In our years of working with managers, we have found some highly educated men and women who are technically and professionally superior but who barely understand how they themselves function. Most of these managers could describe the way they thought they were, but discussions with their employees frequently gave a very different picture. Our self-concepts are frequently overgrown by our ambitions, fears, and circumstances. It is hard to see ourselves objectively. Joe was no different.

His father's success as the senior partner of a powerful law firm had both inspired and depressed Joe. His early desire to write and draw got sidelined as competitive sports was given more approval at the nightly dinner table. Though talk on many subjects was penetrating, argumentative, and fast-paced, activity won the most approval. Joe's father dominated, but his mother's creative wit and people-savvy added spice to the evenings.

By high school graduation, Joe had been persuaded to major in finance and go for an MBA. His mother encouraged him to take some things he enjoyed, like cinematography, creative writing, and graphics. So Joe followed the plan, with finance as the focus and his creative electives as the spice.

Joe scored as an INTJ (introvert, intuitor, thinker, judge). The Myers-Briggs Indicator on style enables a person to identify preferences along the following lines:

Extrovert 53 .... 0 .... 59 Introvert
(Active/Talkative)   (Private/Reserved)

Sensor 67 .... 0 .... 51 Intuitor (N)
(Factual/Realistic)   (Abstract/Imaginative)

Thinker 50 .... 0 .... 50 Feeler
(Cause-effect logic)   (Personal value logic)

Judge 55 .... 0 .... 61 Perceiver
(Decision/Control)   (Adaptation/Flexibility)

Compare Joe's preferences with Ann and Tom's preferences to see how some of the pressure occurred.

Ann   ESFJ   (Extrovert, Sensor, Feeler, Judge)
Joe   INTJ   (Introvert, Intuitor, Thinker, Judge)
Tom   ESTJ   (Extrovert, Sensor, Thinker, Judge)

Extroversion-Introversion

We will compare one dimension at a time to explore possibilities. On extroversion-introversion they scored the following:

Tom (ESTJ)	Ann (ESFJ)	Joe (INTJ)
Extrovert 53 .... 0 .... 59 Introvert		
Tom Ann		Joe
45 **30**		**45**

Both the boss and Ann liked more socializing, more talk, and more interaction than did Joe. In their eagerness to promote him, both Tom and Ann overscheduled activities that would advance Joe's career. Tom insisted that Joe be available four days a week for business lunches. He personally supervised those contacts to see that Joe was continually meeting new people and staying in touch with the "inside network."

Tom encouraged Joe to get to the bank at 7:00 A.M. to have time to spend in the executive dining room to get the "informal briefing." Tom also tried to insist on happy-hour contacts, even though Joe resisted due to his goal of getting home to the family.

Ann's extroverting pressure hit Joe in a different way. Her gregarious nature was considerably blunted by being at home with the children during the day. So when Joe got home, Ann was usually full of plans for evenings that included neighbors, friends, and church activities. Joe was trying to play the game.

Sensing-Intuiting

Tom (ESTJ)	Ann (ESFJ)	Joe (INTJ)
Sensor 67 .... 0 .... 51 Intuitor		
Tom Ann		Joe
59 **49**		**45**

The sensor-intuitor dimension indicates the preferred information-processing style. When Joe, Tom, and Ann went to a party, Tom and Ann were full of information on the way home. They had collected all sorts of factual data at the party. Their conversation focused on who said what, who was dressed appropriately, who was wearing the most elegant symbols of success, and who was connecting with whom. Joe was usually silent, lost in his own thoughts about the interconnectedness of all of those details, looking at the implications and weaving his impressions of the party into a fabric of insight and understanding. He compared information from the past with what he observed at the party that night, and his mind raced ahead into the future to predict what that might mean tomorrow. Both the boss and Ann ribbed Joe about his three long conversations at the party, chiding him for wasting so much time on individuals. They reminded him that socials were for connecting and networking. He thought they were to explore ideas and search for understanding. They jokingly called him the boring, serious one.

Even on the occasional leisure evenings Ann and Joe spent together, her preference for sensing and Joe's preference for intuition caused conflict. As they both tiredly dropped onto the sofa, Joe reached for the television switch and deftly dialed a documentary on pesticide. Ann insisted that he turn off that pessimism and find a comedy or romantic drama. Ann just wanted to sense and enjoy; Joe wanted to learn and explore.

Thinking-Feeling

Tom (ESTJ)		Joe (INTJ)		Ann (ESFJ)
Thinker 50	....	0	....	50 Feeler
Tom	Joe		Ann	
49	**41**		**35**	

The thinker-feeler dimension indicates preferences in decision-making. The thinker usually feels most comfortable with decisions that use a rational problem-solving approach which analyzes the rules or main variables and reaches as fair a decision as possible. The feeler glances at the rules and then identifies the "important values" of the people involved and decides according to personal values.

At the bank, Tom and Joe debate an issue, attack each other's position, regroup, and wrangle until they are satisfied that they have looked at all relevant data. Both men are very bright, and Tom's attention to detail is well matched with Joe's attention to implication and possibility. They are a formidable team.

At home, Joe's preference for time to think things through and keep internal order among his thoughts and feelings is under constant attack by Ann. With a score of 35 as a feeler, Ann likes lots of affection and an ongoing verbal reaffirmation of Joe's love for her. Her need baffles Joe. He cannot understand why she has to be told repeatedly that he loves her. He believes the rationality of his behavior proves that. Once he had even tried to convince her that his faithfulness, hard work, and his spending every moment with her that he wasn't at work should be proof of his love. She became indignant and accused him of being insensitive and unromantic. Ann prefers to feel feelings, while Joe prefers to analyze feelings.

Judging-Perceiving

Tom (ESTJ)   Ann (ESFJ)   Joe (INTJ)

Judge 55 .... 0 .... 61 Perceiver

      Tom   Ann   Joe

      55   **45**   **10**

With all three scoring as judge-controllers, a tug-of-war results. They each have ideas about control, scheduling, and planning. Tom tried to schedule and oversee Joe's activities in the bank. Ann tried to control family activities, and Joe spent most of his time trying to control time so that he could make all of his commitments.

Joe scored 11 as a judge-controller. He liked less structure and more spontaneity than either Ann or Tom. If it weren't scheduled, then Ann and the boss usually wouldn't even consider it.

Early in his marriage, Joe just conceded that there would be no slipping out to a sneak preview at midnight with Ann. If she didn't have it scheduled, she just refused to go, stating, "I don't want to hurry around and go. You know I don't like spur-of-the-moment activities."

Joe's boss had even more rigidity about unscheduled activities. Tom scheduled every morning, lunch, and happy hour to enhance his network somewhere in the city. He could be quite flexible about "where" just as long as the "who" was in his power network plan.

By now, you may be wondering if these three people couldn't see the pattern of their behavior. They saw bits and pieces and kidded about some of it, but they did not see it clearly enough to make better decisions. They were so busy pursuing their own ideas of what they wanted, that little time was spent in identifying the forces that were really running the show. Joe's sudden and unexpected brush with death, however, got their attention.

Tom became so fascinated with the materials that he insisted that all of the bank officers fill out the Myers-Briggs Indicator. He began to think about the long-term health and care of the staff. He tagged thirty of the top players for an intensive team-building training. When they completed the Myers-Briggs, their team showed the following preferences: Out of 30 participants they had 21 introverts, 28 sensors, 30 thinkers, and 27 judge/controllers. Tom began to wonder how many other potential heart attacks were on their way. We assured him that the Myers-Briggs was not an indicator of physical health. Its primary use is to enable people to identify their preferences and then thoughtfully consider the habits and attitudes that are dominating perceptions and judgments. Awareness facilitates better choices.

Both Joe and Ann sat down and carefully explored their differences. They worked hard to understand each other. They began to learn from each other. They discovered that all of us are both introverted and extroverted, sensing and intuiting, thinking and feeling, judge-controlling and perceiving-adapting. The important thing, they realized, was to recognize preferences and develop the potential of the least preferred side of each dimension.

SEVEN STEPS TO DEVELOPING BALANCE

All three of the people in this case began to make some changes. They followed seven steps.

Step 1:	*Attention*	Joe's heart attack got their attention.
Step 2:	*Recognition*	The Myers-Briggs Indicator helped them recognize their patterns.
Step 3:	*Awareness*	Discussion taught them to be aware of the patterns both in themselves and in others.
Step 4:	*Decision*	They each decided to do something about developing their least preferred side. They decided on different guidelines for interaction in the dysfunctional areas.
Step 5:	*Vision*	By seeing the strengths and weaknesses of their preferences, they formed a vision of potential development.
Step 6:	*Commitment*	They made growth and development a number-one priority.
Step 7:	*Action*	They decided on specific daily actions to develop more balance.

Joe's heart attack occurred four years ago. Today he is president of that bank, and Tom Allen is chairman of the board. Ann has opened an office and begun her career. Their individual styles did not stop them, but life became more understandable as they learned how to identify the process of what was happening to them. The more they learned about their own style, the more they learned about others. The once unfathomable mystery of human behavior does have identifiable patterns after all.

Joe was not content to be a manager. He wanted to be a leader too. But first he had some important things to learn. Joe's understanding of his style was the foundation he needed for development of his leadership skills. He paid a price but discovered that balance is the key to his health as well as his path to leadership.

— 2 —

Leadership

In many years of working with organizations, we have learned to respect the word "leader" and to apply it with discrimination. We distinguish clearly between a manager and a leader. We see a manager as a skilled technician in the management basics of planning, organizing, evaluating, supervising, communicating, and coordinating. We've seen managers with good people skills who didn't fit the definition of leader. Barr & Barr uses the term "leader" in this way:

> A LEADER IS MORE FEARLESS, MORE CLEAR, MORE UNLIMITED, MORE WISE, AND MORE COURAGEOUS THAN ANYONE ELSE AROUND.

> A LEADER SEES THE VISION, COMMUNICATES ITS POSSIBILITIES, BELIEVES IN ITS ACHIEVEMENT, INSPIRES OTHERS TO CONTRIBUTE THEIR BEST, MOTIVATES OTHERS TO WANT TO BELONG, STRETCHES AND PUSHES PEOPLE, AND DEMONSTRATES THE CONFIDENCE OF VICTORIOUS ACHIEVEMENT OF THE VISION.

Such a definition leads us to distinguish between true leaders and pseudo leaders. It also leads us to the conclusion that leadership is an ongoing, dynamic process of being fearless, clear, unlimited, wise, and more courageous than anyone else around.

The leader inherits the tests that go with earning the title. People continually test their leaders by questioning and watching for signs of error or weakness. Enemies criticize, try to entrap and destroy leaders. Therefore, true leadership requires the ongoing con-

21

frontation of fears. The leader must come to know them and get comfortable with them. The leader must master those energies to be able to think clearly while experiencing them.

We didn't say the leader eliminates fears; we said, the leader *masters* fears. When the leader's doubts and fears flood through his/her system, the leader does not become off-center. Regardless of the force of the images that are hitting the leader, the vision remains clear, the purpose remains targeted.

Anyone trying to unseat a leader is going to attack or manipulate fears. Hence, it is essential for the leader to do continual, brutal self-examination to maintain clarity and balance. Both fear and power tend to distort perception. The leader must be startlingly clear to avoid such distortion.

The leader must also be clear about personal style and remove the limitations of style preferences that distort interactions. The Myers-Briggs information is a way to identify preferences which could limit leadership capability. One of the most difficult challenges is to get and keep a clear picture of oneself. If you want to lead, you must know your own strengths and weaknesses. A worthy opponent will have already identified them in you. If you are blind to them, then you will be much easier to manipulate.

Think about the way your employees tell you what they think you want to hear. Do you suppose your peers, associates, spouse and even your mother are any less skilled at reading your style preferences? True leadership demands self-knowledge and self-examination. The Myers-Briggs Type Indicator is one way of aiding that process.

To lead, you must search out your own limits and remove them. Identify preferences on each of the dimensions, and then develop the opposite side. By developing your potential you remove the limits of one-sided preference in a dual world.

A wise old retired businessman told us the following:

> You'll know when you are in the presence of a leader. I can't nail it down, but you'll know. When you're with a leader you find yourself standing taller; you'll feel something you didn't know you had sorta *[sic]* turn on inside. You'll start thinking maybe the impossible *is* possible, and before you know it, you're helping to make it possible. You find yourself doing things you didn't think you could. But he knew. He could see the possible in you all along. He will

lead, force or push you until you see it too. Now, that may not be too clear, but just talking about a leader makes me want to be in the thick of it. A leader inspires you and scares the hell out of you at the same time.

If you have ever been in the presence of a leader or had the good fortune to work for one, you probably see and feel what the businessman tried to describe.

CASE STUDY: BALANCED PREFERENCES

The finest leader I know is a complex, brilliant man. I'll call him Lee. I spent a number of years trying to figure out just what style he prefers. Since the Myers-Briggs information has been invaluable as a vertebra around which I can organize the bits and pieces of human behavior, I began to observe him to discover his style.

The longer I worked with him, the more confused I became at identifying his preferences. I saw examples of introversion and extroversion. That seemed normal to me since each of us has both characteristics. I kept waiting to see if I could identify his real preference. After much observing I came to the realization that this man had brought the opposites to balance point; he was comfortable with both introversion and extroversion, with both sensing and intuitive data, with both thinking and feeling decisions, and with both judging and perceiving approaches. I learned much later that this outstanding leader had preferences on the four dimensions, but he had developed the skills of the other side. His preferences comprised his natural style and his skills comprised the other possibilities, and he had become excellent at both. He used whatever was most appropriate for the situation.

Extroversion-Introversion

His ability to maximize both introversion and extroversion amazed me. One example was when we walked out of a six-hour marathon board meeting. People and questions had bombarded us with extroverting energies. We went to his office. An upset employee was waiting for him. Lee quietly listened while demonstrating the introverted capacity to withdraw attention from external surroundings and concentrate intently.

As I watched this interaction, I realized that I was still racing inside. My mind was still scattered with thoughts and images from the board meeting. Though I was disciplining myself to *appear* to be listening intently, my mind was still extroverting. I was impressed with Lee's discipline. He simply brought his concentration to the listening process. The person with the problem began to relax, long before the problem was solved. Lee's genuine interest in listening to the person helped the employee relax. There was no struggle for his attention. The relaxation seemed to begin as the troubled person reacted to the loving gift of being genuinely heard.

Suddenly, I saw real leadership and it didn't look anything like the slick manipulation of image that too many of us have settled for as exemplar leadership. I saw a leader giving time and energy through listening and discussing. I saw a leader giving of himself.

Thinking-Feeling

In thirty minutes I saw a transformation take place in the anxious employee. The lines of worry, the slumped shoulders, the restless body movement, the low energy and the clogged thinking were replaced. As the man walked out the door, his eyes were clear again, he was walking straight, and he had figured out what to do. You probably think that Lee gave him the answer to the problem. He didn't. Lee gave his energy, his concentration, his listening, and his targeted questions to help the person relax and get back in touch with his own ability to think. Lee saw the potential in the young man to solve his own problem. He only needed a bit of directing and stabilizing to help him discover his own solution. Lee showed the balance of thinking and feeling in the way he listened and spoke.

The true leader develops people by enabling them to get in touch with their own strengths. The pseudo leader demands that people see how wonderful s/he is. The pseudo leader would have handled the troubled man quite differently. The pseudo leader would have provided answers and advice. Whatever the man did, he would be continually reminded that he couldn't handle it and had to call on the "big boss." The true leader gives; the pseudo leader takes.

Lee is a true leader, according to our definition. Although he is a natural thinker, he remains open to feeling. The thinker naturally likes to problem-solve. When someone has a problem, the thinker automatically considers solutions. Lee, undoubtedly, had solutions occurring to him as he listened to the troubled employee. He chose to forego the intellectual enjoyment of solving the problem and chose instead to give the employee the growth and enjoyment of discovering his own solution. Through listening and guiding, the leader gave and the follower grew. The real test of leadership is in the work of the follower.

The importance of knowing your preference and of developing the other side of that preference is essential in true leadership. Though Lee is a natural thinker, he also is open to the feeling content of an interaction.

In organizations I have seen people respond out of their own preference and try to force others to use the same one. If Lee had not developed both thinking and feeling, his response to the upset employee would have been quite different. An often observed response is "What's the problem? If you're too upset to tell me the problem, go back to your office until you get it together. Then come back and talk." Too often, I have seen managers demand that upset feelings be denied. They give the strong message that only thinker preference will be tolerated. All other messages are seen as "wrong."

A true leader reads the situation and responds accordingly. Matching the response to the appropriateness of the situation is the key. A true leader gives through guiding the growth of others.

While I was still sorting out mentally the brilliance of the interaction Lee had just had, Sally came into his office. She was cursing and ranting about a customer's stupidity. Rather than listening empathically, Lee interrupted her and said, "Don't waste my time telling me how superior you are to your customer. What do you want from me?" I was shocked at his response. I looked quickly at Sally and saw the startled look on her face. She stopped and was very quiet. Finally, she said, "I'm doing it again, aren't I?" Lee replied, "Yes, you are."

Sally turned toward me and said, "I am trying to change my arrogant attitude toward customers. Lee helped me see the damage my attitude does. I don't even realize when I've become arrogant again. I just get so angry. The moment I start to express it, I just get angrier and angrier."

She turned to Lee and said, "When you asked me what I

wanted from you, I realized that I wanted you to help me stop. Thanks."

One more time I realized that the true leader responds in the way that is best for the growth and development of others. The true leader transcends his/her own preference in order to do what is best for others.

I began to wonder if Lee had also balanced his preference on the sensing-intuiting dimension. The intuitor synthesizes, interprets, and identifies patterns and implications. The intuitor looks at the big picture and its possibilities. The sensor, however, looks at the current picture and today's realities. The sensor preference observes and fills in specific facts and details. Sensors like to act on what is currently available, while intuitors like to act on what might become available. I got my chance to observe Lee's use of both sensing and intuiting.

Sensing-Intuiting

Three young employees had a planning meeting with Lee. They were presenting their marketing plan for one of the departments. As I observed the meeting, I became aware that the three had little grasp of the general business environment.

Lee continually expands employees' ability to see and think. He listened to their presentations and then guided them through a discussion on the influences of the world situation. He painted the economic picture as the background for their business judgment.

Lee began with an intuitive overview explaining that the various sectors of the economy were intricately interlinked. He explained the interdependency of the parts, showing the employees how to think globally while focusing on American business. He described the American business environment as going through great change.

On the American scene, he identified a number of sectors for them to consider: farming, ranching, banking, manufacturing, energy, construction, retail, and bureaucracy. They began to see the big picture as their discussion showed their comprehension.

Next Lee introduced three concepts they would need to consider to interpret the big picture. He talked to them about the overvalued dollar, the trade deficit, and the national debt. These were all terms with which they were familiar, but they did not have a clear picture of how they actually worked. I know that time is vitally important to a busy executive; yet, I watched Lee take the time to work with those employees, to teach them, to be with them. He asked the questions that forced them to use all four dimensions of their style.

He focused on the concept of the overvalued dollar. At that point he moved from the intuitive and began a sensor explanation with details and clarity to help them grasp the abstract concept. He used an analogy of three businessmen: a German, a Japanese, and an American. He explained that the value of the dollar only has meaning when you compare it with other world currencies. He explained: "Let's assume that the Japanese and the American have a similar product to sell to the German. If the American must get $1,000 for his product, he will need the equivalent German marks for the dollars. If it currently takes 50 marks to make up an American dollar but only 30 marks to equal a Japanese yen, the German would realize more value by purchasing the Japanese product." Lee carefully explained that a strong dollar took more of a country's money to purchase the dollar amount that the American businessman had to have in order to make a reasonable profit.

Lee continued the examples, weaving details, implications, and cause-effect logic into the picture: "The American businessman is handicapped in the competitive world market because his American labor costs are among the highest in the world and American parts for his product are also among the highest. In competing against other countries with cheap labor markets, whose parts are probably also cheaper, he is at a disadvantage."

The young employees began to digest the information and began to have a useful picture of the strength or weakness of the American dollar.

Lee then tied the imbalance-of-trade concept to their discussion. Using the sensor skill of moving in a linear fashion through the details, he talked about the trade imbalance. Using his same example of the three businessmen, Lee showed why the German and Japanese were not eager to buy our products. Because of the strong dollar, they were eager to sell us their products because of the strong-dollar buying power in other economies.

Following the theme of competition, Lee explained the current trend of shifting manufacturing bases from America to Third World countries with a plentiful supply of cheap labor. He showed the rationale that embattled American businessmen used to make their decisions to move manufacturing out of America. He showed the sensor decision rationale of staying in business and remaining competitive. Then he showed the intuitive aspect by looking at the long-range implication of such moves.

"Manufacturing jobs have long been a stabilizing part of our communities. The economic impact of manufacturing jobs is highly desirable for community retail stores. Local merchants would rather see manufacturing jobs with their stable and often higher salaries, than many of the service jobs. Comparing a union-wage manufacturing worker and a cook in the local restaurant, the manufacturing job puts more purchasing power into the community than the minimum-wage cook. When manufacturing moves out of the community and out of the country, jobs are lost. Former workers can no longer pay their bills at the grocery store, the gas station, the doctor's office, and the clothing store."

As I watched the three people, I saw them internalize the situation. No longer were they just throwing around terms and talking in an intellectually separated way about trade imbalance. Now they were seeing and feeling the concept. They were seeing the impact of the flight of manufacturing and they were feeling the effect. Lee was activating both their intuitive and sensory awareness of the issues.

"Trade in one sector of the economy affects other sectors. You recall when the dairy farmers got into economic trouble, the federal government 'helped' out," said Lee. "The government further subsidized the dairy farmers by purchasing large numbers of dairy cattle. The government in turn decided to get rid of their newly acquired dairy cattle by selling them to the meat-packing industry at below market value. As a consequence of that action, the price of beef was driven down, placing hardships on ranchers and their beef herds. Thus, the government intervention in the dairy subsidy created hardships on the ranching sector. Dropping beef prices caused ranchers to have difficulty buying feed, fertilizer, equipment, and making bank loan payments."

Lee continued talking to them about farmers acquiring loans on their farms at a time of inflated land values. He supplied details about rising costs of manufactured farm equipment and fertilizer. He showed them how those rising costs were tied to the rising costs of labor, to inflation, to the national debt, and to the trade imbalance.

The three listeners were beginning to see and feel the interconnectedness of the situation and began to identify with the farmers. Their previous tendency to judge the farmers' intelligence for getting into the debt situation changed to empathy as they understood the interdependency.

Lee then linked the farm, ranch, and energy situation to current banking climate. As he described the growing dependency on foreign oil, they began to see that large amounts of American money were leaving this country for those purchases. Small, independent oil companies were being forced out of business because the price of oil had been driven down, thus putting more pressure on banks because of energy exploration loans.

The employees began to make observations and ask questions about the banking crisis and its relationship to inflated land price borrowing, deflated land price loan repayment, oil-based economies, and manufacturing-based economies. Quickly they began to see America's inextricable involvement with Third World countries' debts. They began to see that debts could grow so large that interest-only payments were all the debtor could manage. With no capacity to make principal payments, the debt would quickly reach impossible repayment status. The result would be that banks would have to increase their loan loss reserves, hence diminishing profit and therefore stockholder dividends.

In the unraveling of the complexity, the employees found themselves with a working knowledge of the complex economic concepts. They began to see how the American national debt with its huge interest payments is sucking money out of the public money supply. The government practice of spending more than it takes in has created an enormous drain on the public money supply. With the government borrowing more and more money to pay its budget deficits and interest, the national debt continues to grow.

Quickly, Lee summarized their discussion by reviewing the economic situation. He mentioned psychological pressures with economic impact. He talked of the fear of litigation and rising liability insurance costs that were driving some people out of business. To provide the sensory data, he used the example of a day-care provider who had the principal ingredients of a successful business. She had state-approved facilities, licensed care-givers, lots of customers, five buses for delivering children, and excellent drivers. What she did not have was the money for liability insurance for the day-care services. She went out of business.

Again, Lee had skillfully demonstrated the overall concept of rising liability costs and then tied it to detailed examples of the effect. Using both intuitive and sensory material, the discussion came alive.

Continuing to summarize the psychological and economic pressures, Lee mentioned the drug culture and discussed the economic impact on lost tax revenue, money leaving the country illegally, and the crime involved. "Perhaps the worst impact is the psychological and emotional disturbance that affects our ability to lead responsible, productive lives," he said.

"Understanding today's business environment is vital to our being able to contribute in a positive way. I want you to review your marketing plan by looking at its overall effect, then reviewing the details of making it work. Just as we looked at the big picture and the key concepts in our discussion, I want you to see where your marketing plan fits with the rest of our company, identify the key concepts you are working with, then be tough on the details to make it work. We'll meet again Friday at 10:00 to discuss the plan." The employees walked to the door. I noticed their movement was energetic and their conversation was animated. Could it be that the leader had energized them with possibilities and had frightened them a bit with his expectations?

Judging-Perceiving

I had one more dimension to go in my attempt to unravel the mystery of Lee's style. Is he a judge-controller or a perceiver-adapter? Remember that indicators of judge-controller preference are planning, organizing, controlling, and dominating. There were times when I saw Lee doing all of these things. Just when I thought I had evidence that he was a judge-controller, I saw indicators of perceiver-adapter preferences. Perceivers can go with the flow; they wait to see and then alter the course spontaneously. As you probably suspect, I again found Lee to be balanced between these two opposites.

I asked him about the two opposites and he readily told me that he had a strong preference for judge-controlling. He identified four types of experience that had taught him the wisdom of responding situationally instead of preferentially. His participation on the varsity basketball team, four years in the military, personal love relationships, and years in leadership positions had contributed to his understanding of the value of both. "A true leader must inspire others to achieve, communicate in the way the followers best understand, and empower them to take risks. If I want to lead, I have to do what is best for others and for the accomplishment of the goal," he said. "Many people think being a leader means rank and privilege. That isn't true. Being the leader really means being the servant; it means putting your own needs last and others first. Show me someone who is playing big shot by making others feel small, and I'll show you a power player instead of a true leader. If you want to lead, you have to transcend personal preferences and develop your capacity to introvert and extrovert, intuit and sense, think and feel, judge and perceive. To lead, you must be mature enough to do what is required. Strong belief in something bigger than yourself is the foundation. Personal preference is the communication mechanism."

Developing all eight categories of the Myers-Briggs dimensions is a viable strategy for developing leadership potential. When you think of leadership you have to think of courage to risk, sound judgment, clear perception, and effective skills. Dig deeper than that and you start with a description of the habitual style of the individual.

Studying a manager who chose to cling to his style preferences will help you better understand the theme of balance as the key to leadership.

CASE STUDY: FAILURE TO BALANCE PREFERENCES

Let's look at an executive director of a public agency. He is an intelligent, creative person with positive motives; however, he has very clear preferences and little motivation to reach beyond the comfort zone of his preferences. On the Myers-Briggs Type Indicator, Ted scored as an ENFP (extrovert, intuitor, feeler, perceiver). Ted found the information interesting but was not moved to develop the other side of his preferences. He said, "Yeah, that's pretty much the way I am, all right. I've been that way all my life."

Ted was comfortable with his style of preferences. His comfort blinded him to his fears and weaknesses. Acceptance of preferences is essential to develop a nonguilt base for the development of our dual nature. Ted's decision to be complacent, however, left him with a number of fears: fear of failure, fear of rejection, fear of rational debate, and fear of conflict.

When you look at Ted's career pattern, you see one of perpetual promotion. You might be tempted to agree with Ted's satisfaction with his style, until you take a look at the devastation he left behind when he was promoted. Ted may be the ultimate example of the "Peter Principle." He was promoted beyond his level of competence over and over. He interpreted the promotions as indicators of how good he was and thus avoided confronting his fears and risking the pain of developing his other preferences.

Ted was incompetent as a manager and had not developed the clarity, wisdom, or courage to be a leader. He was just a very nice guy — a heck of a hunter, and socially skilled. I don't believe he knew that his promotions came as ways to get him out of the chaos he caused.

Let's look at Ted's preferences for extroversion, intuition, feeling, and perceiving-adapting (ENFP). There is nothing inherently wrong with any style of preference. Problems occur when those preferences become so strong that they limit perception and judgment.

By Ted's fifty-eighth year, he was executive director of a public agency of 500 employees. The majority of employees were aged twenty-two to thirty-two. This younger work force was 60% white collar and 40% blue collar. They were ambitious and bright. Ted's attitude toward all of them was paternal. He referred to them as "my kids." He took great pride in being a good daddy. When questioned about what he meant by being a good daddy, he smilingly replied, "I mean being friendly, knowing their names, patting them on the back, and telling them they're doing a good job . . . you know, working together like a happy family."

Ted's own words give clues to the preference problems that got him fired. He failed to read his work force accurately. The young professionals were personally insulted by the paternalistic approach. Many of the other workers interpreted his friendly behavior as a "connection" which they could utilize for favors. His eight department chiefs saw the paternalism as an arena for manipulation and intimidation. Thus the department chiefs were in an all-out power struggle, and most of the employees felt caught in the environment of destructive competition for "daddy's favors."

Extroversion-Introversion

Ted's extroversion had turned into an ongoing need to be with people. His continual need for his environment to respond to him became conflicted with his need for affection and approval as a feeler. He needed everyone to approve of him and to give him affection. He could not tolerate bad news. It did not take long for even the newest employee to realize that "you don't tell the old man anything he doesn't want to hear. If you do, you won't even get considered for promotion. You'll be on the old man's unpromotable list because of 'bad attitude.' "

Occasionally, someone would find the game intolerable and would try to give Ted the real picture. I was at a management meeting when one of his department chiefs could no longer keep quiet. Ted was giving one of his messianic endorsements — a mixture of cheerleading, coaching, and evangelistic zeal. One of the chiefs could see the problems that would be created. She spoke up. She quickly offered variables that must be considered: budget constraints, community impact, lack of equipment, and lack of trained personnel.

Ted's face turned beet-red as he jumped out of his chair and began pacing wildly around the room. Without addressing the issues or the chief, he launched a tirade on some unknown offender. "I am sick and tired of negative attitudes. Where are the creative thinkers? Where are the can-do people? Where are the people with courage to do something different? Where would Bear Bryant have been if he didn't have the courage to push his boys into tough situations?"

At that point, he turned to the chief who had raised the question and said, "Now, Sandra, I'm not talking about you. It just reminded me of the people around here who need to get on or off the wagon. I want all of you to go back to your department and keep an eye out for anyone in your department who isn't pulling his own weight. We need to weed out those with a bad attitude. They can just find somewhere else to work. Meeting dismissed!"

What effect do you think that interaction had on the staff? Everyone at the meeting knew that Ted was releasing his anger at Sandra. He did not have the clarity nor the courage to claim his anger. Instead, he pretended to focus it on "unknown offenders." One of the department chiefs competing with Sandra for a new piece of equipment interpreted the event as his opportunity to get it. He knew that Sandra would be out of favor for a while.

Sensing-Intuiting

The intuitive preference reinforced Ted's preference to gloss-over issues. He refused to look at details. He refused to look at the facts of a situation. He refused to see things as they were; instead, he rearranged them in his mind into what he wanted them to be. He refused to allow his sensor abilities to feed him the real situation. Ted was continually chasing the possible with no understanding of the probable.

Thinking-Feeling

Ted's extroversion and sensitivity to feeling kept him constantly alert for any signs of rejection. Thus he interpreted any type of debate as disagreement and rejection. He used his intuitive preference to keep a long-term score card on indicators of dislike for him. He had become so needy that he interpreted the following as indicators of dislike: an employee failing to smile at him, anyone raising an uncomfortable point, anyone who brought him a problem that upset him, anyone failing to remember his birthday, anyone not getting along with everyone, anyone heard challenging his decisions, and anyone not attending the many social events he arranged for the agency.

At this point you are probably ready to argue that this guy can't be real. I assure you he is. The dynamics of his political connections, his sportsmen network, his surface nice personality, his charm at manipulating people, and his lack of conscious, malicious intent formed quite a formidable power base.

His own preference for affection and cooperation turned into domination of his organization. His preferences and his potency limited debate, suppressed open conflict, discouraged creativity, encouraged manipulation, demanded compliance, and dictated acceptance of his distorted reality if an employee wanted to succeed.

Ted used his position as director to orchestrate an environment to stroke and defend his egoic preferences. Since his focus was on himself, one of his chiefs became the power player with whom to deal. While Ted guarded his own feel-good, George used his position to cause a lot of feel-bad.

George had maneuvered a less savvy chief out of an office next to Ted's office. He also had gotten control of two-thirds of the agency budget, 325 of 500 personnel, and control of the "old man."

Judging-Perceiving

Ted's perceiving-adapting nature coupled with his need for people to like him created a perpetual desire to say "yes" to requests from any of his "kids." Various employees or chiefs would go to Ted and ask for something. Ted could get so completely focused on controlling the interaction to a positive feel-good for himself that he usually agreed to the request.

George, next door, could usually hear through the thin partition of the wall the request being made. If the request involved anything he wanted, George went into Ted's office after the person left. He was one of the more skilled manipulators. He complimented Ted, asked his advice on some irrelevant issue, and worked on Ted until he saw the body relax and the evidence of feel-good in Ted's demeanor. George could almost mesmerize Ted. He was so skilled that Ted could completely forget that what he just promised to George had already been promised to someone else. George could get the approval and then act quickly to coopt the request. If the request involved equipment, George would have his staff move the equipment immediately before the other chief could act.

I watched George manipulate the director repeatedly. George became very arrogant about his ability to do so. He had convinced the director that he was the best and toughest and most dependable son on the job. He repeated to the director his total loyalty. George further manipulated Ted by staying alert to the issues that upset Ted. When George detected signs of upset, he would go in and tell Ted to just forget about it. George vowed to take care of the problem: "Just put it out of your mind. That's what you pay me to do. I'm your trouble-shooter. That's why I'm here."

Ted usually felt such gratitude to George for making the pain go away and for restoring his illusion that everything was wonderful again that Ted actually gave George the organization. Ted could then go back to his illusion that he was a good daddy and everyone was cooperating and there were no problems.

A true leader would never measure his success by the absence of problems.

Ted's refusal to take responsibility for his extroversion caused the organization real problems. He refused to take the introverted in-depth probe into issues; he chose instead to gloss-over issues. The positive use of extroversion allows a person to read cues from the environment, while the positive use of introversion allows a person to concentrate on understanding the cues. Ted side-stepped any responsibility to do either.

SUMMARY

Ted's refusal to develop his analytical abilites of the thinker preference threw him into the vulnerability of too much feeling. He decided employees' merits on agreeable-disagreeable variables. If people made him feel good, they were agreeable and therefore good employees. If they made him feel bad, they were disagreeable and therefore were bad employees. He let his heart dictate and refused to discipline himself to use thinker thoroughness in assessing an issue.

The perceiving-adapting preference had developed into avoidance of decision, avoidance of responsibility, and abandonment of authority. He refused to develop the judge-controlling preference to take a planned, organized, responsible approach to his job. Ted just went with the flow of the feel-good and exercised judge-controlling to make feel-bad go away.

Compare the leadership approach the case-study leader Lee uses by developing all eight categories of the Myers-Briggs dimensions with the preferences of Ted. Ted's refusal to develop the strengths of both introversion and extroversion, sensing and intuiting, thinking and feeling, judging and perceiving caused management problems, personal problems, and organizational problems.

— 3 —

Communication:
Extroversion-Introversion

Is it possible to read people accurately? Can you accurately predict people's responses?

We believe that people-reading is a skill of reading people's patterned responses. We have to learn to see the pattern instead of the singular action. Common sense tells us that so much information bombards us continuously that we are incapable of responding to all of it with clearcut, conscious choices. Millions of bits of information hit our system, but most are processed below the level of consciousness; therefore, predispositions and preferences play an important role in processing the information. Much of this complicated process of sorting information is affected by our individual preferences. We have habitual ways of seeing and thinking.

The Myers-Briggs helps us identify those preferences that greatly affect perception and judgment. Learning the implications of those preferences is essential to accurately reading human behavior. As we become aware of the limits and strengths of our own preferences, we by comparison study those who don't share our preferences.

Earliest civilization found a need to understand, predict, and control people's actions. In our most advanced culture, we still share the need to understand each other in order to sustain life. The Greeks' approach is as valid today as it was when they advised "know thyself." You must know yourself, if you want to truly know others.

37

The Myers-Briggs Type Indicator is one of the most useful, nonjudgmental ways of "knowing thyself." It helps us identify the preferences that shape the way we behave. Those preferences produce patterns of behavior that show consistent threads of what otherwise might look like random choice. The four dimensions of attitude and function help to unravel the mystery of human behavior.

Managers today are continually asked to do more with less. Not only does the manager have to rethink the work, but s/he also has to "relook" at the people doing the work. Managers are now expected to develop more of people's potential. What was originally a manager's job is now replete with leadership expectations. Many people who succeeded as managers will fail as leaders if they do not understand people and do not know how to motivate and inspire them.

When people problems erupt, look for the principal field of conflict. We found that most people problems explode over differences of communication, information, judgment, or control.

Communication differences on extroversion-introversion can show you where to look to unravel causes of conflict. Information differences in sensor and intuitor preference can cause conflict. Judgment differences between thinker and feeler preference can cause major struggles. Control differences between judging and perceiving can develop into power struggles. Let's look at each of these dimensions to see characteristics, strengths, weaknesses, and strategies for development.

EXTROVERSION-INTROVERSION AND COMMUNICATION

Communication is a way of viewing events. It is unceasing and has no definable beginning or ending. Though we meet someone for the first time, they may trigger past impressions, feelings, and thoughts. We don't get to start fresh. Each communicator is in a continuous state of monitoring and interpreting impressions.

Communication is an interpretation process. We have a tremendous capacity to edit, rearrange, omit, judge, and interpret the messages we receive. That interpretation process is influenced by our preferences of extroversion or introversion.

The truth is that we are both introverted and extroverted. But in most of us, one of those is preferred and controls more of our behavior. Dr. Carl Jung explains:

When we consider the course of human life, we see how the fate of one individual is determined more by the objects of his interest (extrovert), while in another it is determined more by his own inner self, by the subject (introvert). Since we all swerve rather more towards one side or the other, we naturally tend to understand everything in terms of our own type . . . . In respect of one's own personality one's judgment is as a rule extraordinarily clouded. (p. 3, *Psychological Types*)

We both speak and listen through our introverted or extroverted preference. If you have not already begun to make conscious adjustment for the clouding effect on your judgment, you will see the world through your own bias.

An extrovert prefers people, activities, and the external environment. The extrovert is largely energized by stimuli from the external environment. This person's attention flows outward to people, objects, and activities to maximize interaction. S/he perceives and judges from this perspective predominantly.

An introvert prefers privacy and the inner world of ideas, beliefs, and ordered existence. Introverts are energized by internal stimuli of order and meaning; their attention flows inward toward the private world of ideas. The introvert withdraws attention from the external world in order to balance and establish internal order. S/he perceives and judges primarily from this point of view.

These two preferences create much misunderstanding. The extrovert finds meaning principally from interacting with the external world, while the introvert finds meaning principally from withdrawing from the external world.

Dr. Jung described this difference in the following way:

The peculiar nature of the extravert [translator's spelling] constantly urges him to expend himself in every way, while the tendency of the introvert is to defend himself against all demands from outside, to conserve his energy by withdrawing it from objects, thereby consolidating his own position . . . . The one achieves its end by a multiplicity of relationships, the other by monopoly. (p. 332, *Psychological Types*)

His [extravert] whole consciousness looks outward because the essential and decisive determination always comes from outside . . . . His interest and attention are directed to ob-

jective happenings, particularly those in his immediate environment. Not only people but things seize and rivet his
attention . . . . The actions of the extravert are recognizably
related to external conditions.(p. 334)

. . . he [introvert] is strongly influenced by ideas, though
his ideas have their origin not in objective data but in his
subjective foundation. He will follow his ideas like the extravert, but in the reverse direction: inwards and not out-
wards. Intensity is his aim, not extensity. (p. 383)

It remains an enigma to the extravert how a subjective
standpoint can be superior to the objective situation. He
inevitably comes to the conclusion that the introvert is
either a conceited egoist or crack-brained bigot. The introvert certainly lays himself open to these suspicions, for his
positive, highly generalizing manner of expression, which
appears to rule out every other opinion from the start, lends
countenance to all the extravert's prejudices. Moreover the
inflexibility of his [the introvert's] subjective judgment, setting itself above all objective data, is sufficient in itself to
create the impression of marked egocentricity. (p. 377)

Dr. Jung is using the word "objective" judgment to mean
"having to do with a known or perceived object, not a mental
image or idea." He explains the extrovert's tendency to draw
meaning from the external world. He uses the word "subjective"
judgment of the introvert to mean "of or resulting from the feelings
of the subject, or person thinking, rather than the attributes of the
object thought of."

The extrovert is greatly influenced by the external world and
the introvert is influenced by the internal world. Let's look at some
of the problems that difference creates.

DIFFERENCES BETWEEN EXTROVERTS AND INTROVERTS CAN CAUSE PROBLEMS

When asking extroverts what they disliked about working with
introverts, we received the following comments:

"They [introverts] are too secretive."

"You never know what they are thinking."

"They are too slow. They take too long to give you an answer."

"They are boring."

"They don't give you enough feedback."

"They are terrible brainstormers."

"They are nonspontaneous . . . too careful."

"They are too methodical."

"They already have their minds made up about things. You can't get them to change their minds."

"They seem to accept our solution, then go away and pick it apart."

"They have hidden agendas."

"They only show us their best side. They seem afraid to risk being real. Everything seems so calculated and studied."

"We know the information is in them, but we can't get to it."

"They are too quiet . . . too reserved . . . hold things in too much."

"They seem too insecure to speak up. They seem slow."

"They won't share their feelings, and that means they don't trust us."

When asking introverts what they disliked about working with extroverts, they gave us the following comments:

"They [extroverts] are pushy, obnoxious, and domineering at times."

"They are too loud and boisterous."

"They talk without thinking."

"You can't depend on what they say. They talk about things as if they are going to do them and then they don't."

"They don't listen much; they are too busy talking, or thinking about what they are going to talk about next."

"They are intrusive. They don't respect privacy."

"They talk too much . . . and frequently don't know what they are talking about . . . but seem to get off on the sound of their own voices."

"They are so into their own thing, they are frequently insensitive."

"They wander off the subject."

"They try to draw us out and then interrupt us when we do try to talk."

"Extroverts are in continual launch mode."

These comments came from work groups located in various parts of the country. The comments carried these same general prejudices whether we were working with bankers, lawyers, child-care workers, criminal justice professionals, business people, military officers, or civil servants. The differences between extroverts and introverts can be an ongoing source of conflict if they are not understood and adjusted. Many of the irritations just mentioned are processed below the level of consciousness. As people in our groups began to talk about the differences, they became aware of past people problems that involved extrovert-introvert patterns of communication.

The following characteristics are basic differences between the extroverted and introverted preferences.

EXTROVERT	INTROVERT
Outside world	Inner world
People, action, things	Ideas, thoughts, meanings
Prefers interaction — active	Prefers reflection — reflective
Usually talkative and outgoing	Usually quiet and reserved
Sociable with many friends — refers to others as friends	Introspective with a few close friends — discriminates clearly between acquaintance and friend
Tends to like meeting new people	Tends to postpone meeting new people
Tends to seek new experiences	Tends to avoid new experiences
Sociable	Territorial
External events	Internal reactions
Tends to expand rather than conserve — expansive	Tends to consolidate, defend and protect — controls personal disclosure and interaction
Reacts to stress primarily by increasing activity	Reacts to stress primarily by decreasing activity
Energized by activity	Energized by depth and intimacy

In looking at the differences in preference, it is easy to see how people irritate each other in the work setting. The extrovert deals with space, time, territory, and interaction differently from the introvert. A leader of people needs to manage people dynamics wisely.

EXTROVERT-INTROVERT
USE OF SPACE AND TERRITORY

The extrovert is expansive and expressive. S/he tends to expand into other people's space physically, mentally, and emotionally. The extrovert usually moves with more vitality than the introvert. Willingly expending energy is part of the extroverted nature; thus, animated speaking, brisk movement, and continuous action is natural.

Extroverted managers communicate similar patterns when they are talking to us about their use of space. They tend to want plenty of outer space so they can move freely. They usually like to have an office space located near or in the center of the action. They like to see what's happening. One manager said, "I don't want too much furniture in my office fencing me in — I want to be able to move in and out easily. I like to get out of my office to see what's going on."

Extroverted managers told us that they liked the concept of managing by wandering around. They wanted to be free to move easily, and the concept seemed to be an endorsement of their natural propensity for movement. They also said they liked to spread out when they work. They seemed to prefer large tables and plenty of space when they were working on something; in case someone else wandered in, they could put them right to work. The overall pattern that we found was extroverted managers who saw the satisfaction of management coming from the opportunity for interaction.

One extrovert said, "I want my own parking space at work so I don't waste time getting from my car to where the action and the people are. I like my office to have windows so I can see what's going on."

Introverted managers told a very different story. The dominant pattern was preference for a quiet, private office, away from the noisy interaction of the organization. Most of them agreed that they liked to work with their doors closed when they were concentrating. They rarely wandered around the organization. When they left their offices, they had a specific purpose. Once it was achieved, they tended to go directly back to their offices.

The strong preference for privacy came out clearly. The introverted managers wanted interpersonal space as well as physical. "I resent personal questions. I am here to do a job, not get into my personal life," said a man who scored 41 on the introversion dimension. Others added these comments:

> "I don't like a lot of clutter. I want clean visual space as well as interpersonal white space."

> "I want my own space; I strongly resist anyone trying to control my space."

> "It really irritates me for someone to take something from my desk."

> "I like to be the one to invite others into my space — I don't want others to impose themselves in my space. I don't want to be invaded."

> "I dislike drop-in company; they should be courteous enough to call in advance."

> "I tend to pull my chair back to get more space when talking to someone new or someone who's coming on too hard."

EXTROVERT-INTROVERT INTERACTION TIME

The amount of preferred interaction time varied greatly between the extroverts and introverts scoring 20 or higher on their preference. The extroverts expressed a desire for "lots of interaction time with only an occasional time alone." Just the reverse was expressed by the introverts.

The extrovert has a tendency to talk in order to sort out experience. Talking to others helps the extrovert sort out what s/he is thinking. This tendency to talk to others about something the extrovert is considering causes some difficulty in the work setting. The extroverted manager tends to talk over ideas. If talking to an introvert, the introvert is likely to hold the extrovert responsible for doing what they talked about. The extrovert, however, may talk to five other people about the idea. In each conversation the extrovert is focusing what s/he really thinks about the idea. The extrovert explores possibilities through conversation. The introvert doesn't always recognize that process and therefore holds the extrovert responsible for what the introvert interpreted as agreement on a course of action. One introvert stated, "You know extroverts lie alot. I wish they would tell me which of their ideas I can really count on them to carry out." Unless the introvert is willing to take responsibility for really understanding extroversion, then confusing discussion for decision will continue to cause problems.

One introverted department head was angry about a perceived betrayal by one of the other department heads. The introvert said, "At the meeting last week you said you were going to go to Phoenix and meet with the customer and get the project set up. We set our work plans with that in mind and now I find that you have no intention of going. I can't seem to count on you to do what you say you will." The extrovert responded, "Just a minute. We were exploring possibilities and I said I could go to Phoenix. Afterward I talked to Harry and he said we could arrange a meeting here in our offices and take a different approach. That sounded like a better idea." The extrovert was still discussing possibilities when the introvert interpreted decision and commitment.

The introvert likes to go away and think through a course of action. S/he prefers time and space to think things out internally, then selectively present to others what s/he wants to share of the thought process. The introvert thinks it out while the extrovert talks it out.

Extroverts like to interact with a number of people but get bored easily if "nothing is going on." Rarely do they like to spend too much time with the same people. The more variety the better, is often the motto. Extroverts like to interact, to discuss cases, issues, or problems with others. They accept the fact that there is little time to get to know a subject or person in depth, so they tend to sample more than savor.

By contrast, introverts like in-depth interaction, insisting on quality time for important issues or people. Otherwise, they prefer interaction to be short and to the point. If interaction is not "meaningful," then the introvert tries to avoid it. They have low tolerance for "nonpurposeful interaction." Rarely can they tolerate "small talk." Introverts prefer well-planned interaction time. They do not like drop-ins — it's an invasion of privacy. These attitudes frequently lead others to see introverts as "snobbish, selfish, and hard to get to know."

Introverts tend to be quiet until they are ready to interact, and then it is usually with people of their choice. They tend to enjoy one-to-one conversations rather than group interactions. Being around many people or around one person for too long causes stress. They tend to like short interactions, followed by rest and private time, and they prefer to avoid day-long meetings where someone else is controlling interaction guidelines.

EXTROVERT-INTROVERT ATTITUDES TOWARD NOISE

Extroverts and introverts tend to view noise differently. Extroverts usually define noise as anything that interrupts action or conversation that the extrovert is controlling. They tend to view controlled noise as security; too much quiet makes the extrovert uneasy. Negative noise is defined as noise that is repetitive and nonhuman, such as crickets, machine noises, dogs barking, cats screaming. If the sound is attached to human interaction, extroverts usually don't label it noise — they call it life.

Introverts define noise as anything that intrudes into the inner world of concentration. One introvert explained, "I hate sudden unexpected noises. I don't want sudden, unwanted intrusions of any kind . . . noise, people, telephone ringing, someone else's music." Negative noise is anything that interrupts the introvert's control over his/her own setting. If someone else's noise is loud and interruptive, then the introvert may choose to fight the noise with noise that s/he can control personally. The introvert might play music where s/he can control the volume and use it to drown-out noises that someone else controls — like setting a backfire to kill the raging fire.

Some typical comments from introverts are:

"I don't like interruptions that break concentration."

"I don't like noise; it gets on my nerves."

"If a person's office is too noisy, I just leave and come back later when it is calm enough to work."

"I hate for others to impose their music on me; I want to choose my own."

"Quiet please, I have sensitive ears. If I can't stop their noise, I tune them out internally."

Introverts report a much stronger irritability quotient from noise than do extroverts.

EXTROVERT-INTROVERT USE OF LEISURE

Extroverts and introverts take two separate paths to balancing and managing leisure and relaxing.

Extroverts look for something fun to do with other people. They like to get together with others and do something. They talk about enjoyable, happy, refillable kinds of activities that restore their energy and enthusiasm for life. They don't want hassles; they want energizing interaction.

Extroverts report preferences for leisure that include active sports. Most frequently named leisure activities include camping, and team sports, such as bowling, softball, baseball, volleyball, basketball, and football. Also cited were dancing, people games, cards, aerobics, biking with friends, movies with happy endings, comedies, and music concerts.

Introverts look for private time. They like to spend time alone or with one or two well-known others who do not require relationship building or tending actions from the introverts. Most frequently named leisure activities are reading, quiet dinners, great conversations, gardening, cooking, jogging, hiking, fishing, sailing, movies. They reported preferring leisure to be free of competition. "I want to relax and slow down the pace," one introvert said. "I like to have time to exercise my own priorities . . . . I want to do my thing without meeting someone else's expectations." Another person responded, "Leisure is my time. I want no interruptions. I like quiet time to read, think, and plan."

One management group with extroverts and introverts stated that they liked to go dancing. It sounded like a match — at last. A little more probing uncovered the different approaches the two preferences took. The introverts described their ideal evening of dancing as going to their favorite club and getting a table that was far enough away from the music and the dance floor to allow good conversation as well as dancing. The extroverts clearly signaled that the evening just described sounded very boring. Their description of an ideal evening of dancing included dancing at more than one disco and meeting as many people as possible. The idea of getting a table was purely a functional place to leave their glasses while they were meeting people and dancing. They didn't want to sit down. They wanted to keep dancing and keep moving to see who was there.

Introverts agreed that being around family after work is acceptable and even desirable, but rarely did they want to expend the energy to be around someone new at the end of a busy work day. Work used up most of their extroverting energies, so they liked privacy after work. One introvert said, "I love it when my spouse goes on a trip, so I can have the privacy of the house all to myself. It feels wonderful."

I sometimes think about a valley filled with people and activity as the natural habitat of the extrovert; whereas, a work cozy cave with a well-guarded entrance might be the natural habitat of the introvert.

EXTROVERT-INTROVERT BEHAVIORS

In our management workshops, we ask extroverts and introverts to identify what they like about each other, what they dislike, and what advice they would give each other for improving communication. We have reviewed some of the ideas that they dislike. Let's look at some of the characteristics they value about each other.

EXTROVERTS	INTROVERTS
Make quick decisions	Make well thought-out decisions
Brainstorming capability	Have concentration depth
Gather information quickly	Gather information thoroughly
Straightforward	Responsible, in-depth opinions
Talk easily	Use discretion in talking
Stimulate communication	Focus on subject matter at hand and bring talk back to the topic
Don't mind interruptions	Longer attention span
Good in spontaneous response	Persuasive with sound logic
Able to switch gears easily	Tenacious . . . serious . . . focused
Good at group social interaction	Good at one-to-one interaction
Good at stimulating ideas	Good at developing ideas
Enthusiasm and energy level	Calmness and quiet
Instigate action	Keep confidences

As groups begin to think about the differences between extroverts and introverts, the strengths of both begin to come out. Appreciation for differences is essential for teamwork. A leader utilizes the strengths of each, knowing just the right mix of styles to maximize productivity.

One extrovert said, "You know both of us are lovable. Extroverts are the poodles constantly dancing around and jumping up and down for attention and the introverts are the basset hounds calmly waiting for someone to notice their worth."

When groups of extroverts and introverts were asked to give each other advice about communication, they each had practical suggestions.

EXTROVERTS' ADVICE TO INTROVERTS FOR COMMUNICATION
1. Be assertive.
2. Express your ideas.
3. Show your emotion — it's okay to let others see you as human.
4. Be friendly . . . talk more.
5. Be open-minded.
6. Be more up-beat . . . show a more lively nature.
7. Invite us to an activity once in awhile . . . don't make us do all the arrangements.
8. Don't take things too seriously.
9. Smile more . . . you are hard to approach.
10. Be more playful . . . don't worry about what others think.
11. Give more information on where you are on an issue.
12. Tell me if you like or dislike what I'm saying.
13. Don't judge me as frivolous just because I'm extroverted.
14. Be flexible.

INTROVERTS' ADVICE TO EXTROVERTS FOR COMMUNICATION
1. Respect my privacy . . . don't take up my space.
2. Don't put us in the spotlight.
3. Don't demand an immediate response. Give us the information and let us have time to digest it . . . give us time to answer.
4. Tone down . . . don't overwhelm us with your bluster.
5. Pay closer attention to what we are saying.
6. Give us more facts and less small talk.
7. Help us feel more comfortable by not judging us as inferior . . . remember that not everyone acts the same.

8. Don't betray something we told you in confidence.
9. Learn to listen. Be more understanding of other people's need to express themselves . . . Just because we won't fight you for center stage doesn't mean that we don't have something to say.
10. Put your brain in gear before your mouth takes off.
11. Be patient . . . it takes longer for us to express ourselves.
12. Don't patronize us.
13. Let us know which ideas you are really serious about and that you genuinely are committed to follow through.
14. Don't judge me as dull just because I'm quiet.
15. Follow through when we agree to do something. You seem to be always looking for a better offer. It seems as if you will work with me if you can't find someone more interesting.

Both extroverts and introverts seem to be saying, "Why aren't you more like me? I could understand you better."

Recognizing differences is the first step, accepting differences is the second step, and developing skills for your least preferred side is the crucial third step.

STRATEGY FOR INTROVERTS TO IMPROVE COMMUNICATION WITH EXTROVERTS

REMEMBER: Extroverts are *social* and *active*.
Extroverts are mainly focused on the external environment.

SOCIAL
1. Give feedback.
2. Show interest, emotion, and involvement.
3. Don't withdraw.
4. Open up . . . respond more both verbally and nonverbally.
5. Suspend your annoyance with "nonpurposeful" talk and allow value to come from the process of interacting rather than the quality of ideas exchanged.

ACTIVE
1. Respond quickly.
2. Be spontaneous.
3. Don't talk too long at one time . . . extroverts prefer short bursts rather than long monologues.
4. Occasionally invite an extrovert to an active event.

STRATEGY FOR EXTROVERTS TO IMPROVE COMMUNICATION WITH INTROVERTS

REMEMBER: Introverts are *private, different,* and *serious.*

PRIVATE
1. Respect privacy . . . Avoid asking personal questions that invade private psychological space . . . Don't use their things without permission . . . Don't invade their physical space. Respect their time.
2. Don't put introverts suddenly in the spotlight . . . they prefer to plan ahead if they need to perform a spotlight role.
3. Give introverts as much time to think about ideas or decisions as you can allow.
4. Don't repeat what an introvert told you in confidence . . . Remember: most of the time the introvert is talking to you specifically and may not want his/her words repeated generally . . . Introverts and extroverts are very different about what they consider private.
5. Ask for specific information you need . . . don't assume the introvert will give it, unless asked.

DIFFERENT
1. Norms of human behavior are principally set by extroverts. Don't judge introverts to be inferior because they are unlike the majority.
2. Slow down . . . adjust your energy to a calmer level if you want an introvert's genuine response.

SERIOUS
1. Think before you speak . . . introverts may be intolerant with casual exploration of ideas . . . may judge brainstorming as irrational thought.
2. Give more substantive information and less small talk.
3. Be responsible for letting introverts know when you are just considering ideas for discussion and when you are deciding.
4. Identify clearly which actions you intend to follow through . . . thus, allowing clearer expectations.
5. Pay close attention to what introverts are saying and doing . . . they tend to give subtle signals that are easy to overlook by extroverts.

LEADERSHIP REQUIRES DEVELOPMENT

Your natural preferences for introversion or extroversion may be strong. If you remain stuck in a strong preference with little or no tolerance for the other side, you will remain cut off from your potential. Leading people requires you to accurately read them and know how to develop their potential to grow for their own satisfaction and to produce for the organization.

> Balancing Style = Leadership Enhancement

— 4 —

Information: Sensor-Intuitor

Two people can observe the same event and abstract two very different kinds of information. The sensor sees the details of the event, while the intuitor sees the relationships and patterns within the event and may link the event to other happenings.

The Myers-Briggs Indicator identifies two ways of perceiving and processing information. The *sensor* perceives the world principally through the five body senses and prefers facts that can be immediately proven. The *intuitor* perceives the world principally through the intuition to see the overall picture. Intuition integrates bits and pieces of stored data to form patterns and suggest possibilities. As individuals, we use both processes but have a favorite that we use and trust more.

Sensing is defined by Briggs and McCaulley as one of two kinds of perception.

Sensing (S) refers to perceptions observable by way of the senses. Sensing establishes what exists. Because the senses can bring to awareness only what is occurring in the present moment, persons oriented toward sensing perception tend to focus on the immediate experience and often develop characteristics associated with this awareness such as enjoying the present moment, realism, acute powers of observation, memory for details, and practicality. (p. 12, *Myers-Briggs Manual*)

Intuitive perception is defined as the other kind of perception.

Intuition (N) refers to perception of possibilities, meanings, and relationships by way of insight . . . . Intuitions may come to the surface of consciousness suddenly, as a "hunch" the sudden perception of a pattern in seemingly unrelated events, or as a creative discovery . . . . Intuition permits perception beyond what is visible to the senses, including possible future events. Thus, persons oriented toward intuitive perception may become so intent on pursuing possibilities that they may overlook actualities. They may develop the characteristics that can follow from emphasis on intuition and become imaginative, theoretical, abstract, future oriented, or creative. (p. 12, *Myers-Briggs Manual*)

Intuitive perception is insight gained without conscious reasoning. Sensing perception relies on a "simple and immediate sense-impression." (p. 367, Jung's *Psychological Types*)

"Sensing (S) seeks the fullest possible experience of what is immediate and real. Intuition (N) seeks the broadest view of what is possible and insightful." (p. 13, *Myers-Briggs Manual*)

SENSING PREFERENCE

Sensing perception uses the five senses as receptors of sensory stimuli to provide information about the current situation. Managers who prefer sensing above intuiting have a different way of looking at the world than intuitors. Sensors usually have keen observation abilities with excellent memory for details. They are usually grounded in realism and may be annoyed by someone who speculates about tomorrow. Their practical nature keeps them focused on today, since their five senses are processing the world around them at the moment. Tomorrow hasn't arrived yet, so why focus on it?

Sensors' preferences usually produce an appreciation for structured ways of doing things. They prefer structured tasks with clear operating procedures. Step-by-step approaches are clearly laid out and give sensors comfort in the steady, linear movement of the task. This approach allows the sensor to clearly measure what has already been done and the steps of the work yet to be accomplished.

Structure feels safe and orderly to sensors. Even though some of the steps may be quite difficult, the structured, step-by-step process relieves sensor anxiety about what is expected and the planned way of fulfilling the expectation.

Sensors also prefer more structured ways of learning that involve hands-on kinds of application. They prefer workshops instead of seminars or lectures, application instead of paper-pencil measures, clear and precise instructions instead of open-ended ones, efficient materials instead of creative, interesting ones. Sensors like direct experience in learning, rather than reading or listening.

The most trustworthy information given to sensors is that which comes through the five senses. Their own experience is more trustworthy than information other people tell them, since their main validation of information is their own senses. Expect sensors to question your viewpoint.

As natural pleasure lovers, sensors are usually highly attuned to the sensory factors of a situation. Sense impressions take priority in their consciousness, and they focus much attention on observing the external environment. They can become so focused on observing that they have little energy to use on imagination. They can become imitators of other people by overvaluing what other people possess, do, and think. Sensors have a tendency to become too focused on status symbols as physical measures of who they are. Sensors tend to be more contented than intuitive types. Enjoyment and pleasure are important to sensors. Their five senses and the focus on the present combine to make them well armed to enjoy the world. Comfort, luxury, pleasure, and enjoyment are part of the consumer-of-life approach of sensors.

Sensors value action. What they see you doing is more proof than what they hear you saying. And more importantly, what they see you doing right now carries much more weight than what you say you are going to do in the future. They like action with concrete results and immediate feedback. Their practical nature triggers a distrust of ideas that have not been tried with a track record to indicate their viability. Sensors are interested in what is practical and immediately workable. They are called the doers of the organization, the backbone of the company, since they prefer to work determinedly and methodically through tasks until the desired outcome is reached.

Ask sensors to try something they have not experienced and

you may find real resistance. If they have no direct experience with the idea, they tend to resist and take a negative stance toward it. Theoretical thinking is more difficult for sensors since they prefer experiential thinking where tests of ideas can be inferred from direct or previous experience. Sensors are results-oriented and grow impatient with too much planning and conceptualizing. They want to get their hands on it and get moving.

Perhaps it's the step-by-step, linear approach of sensors that gives them the tendency to produce steadily in regular, rhythmic work cycles. They tend to work with routinized work habits. Since action is one of their most important means of expression, they tend to want quick decisions, short or no meetings, minimum planning, and swift assembling of work materials. Sensors value the bottom line, the number of boxes filled today, the amount of profit this month, and the workplace today. Projections, trends, analysis, and organizational development take a back seat to the work that has to be done today.

Sensors at their best are clear and accurate readers of the facts in the immediate situation. They are usually capable of accurate detail and awareness of the reality of the physical situation.

Sensors and intuitors see the world differently. They integrate information in different ways. They value different kinds of information. Sensors are astute about the sense-impression of the observed situation, while intuitors are astute about the overall situation and implications. Sometimes they can have real difficulty communicating with each other. When trust and respect exist between these two types, they both work harder to understand the difference in their perspectives and expand their tolerance for another way of seeing. Communication at its worst between these two degenerates into sensors seeing intuitors as "weirdos with off-the-wall ideas" and intuitors seeing them as "unimaginative stuck-in-the-mud" types.

Dr. Jung spoke about the potential conflict between the sensing and intuiting perspective.

> The primary function of intuition is simply to transmit images, or perceptions of relations between things . . . . These images have the value of specific insight which have a decisive influence on action whenever intuition is given priority . . . . Thinking, feeling, and sensation are then largely repressed, sensation being the one most affected, because as

the conscious sense function, it offers the greatest obstacle to intuition. Sensation is a hindrance to clear, unbiased, naive perception; its intrusive sensory stimuli direct attention to the physical surface, to the very things round and beyond which intuition tries to peer. (pp. 366–367, Jung's *Psychological Types*)

This struggle between sensing and intuiting perceptions goes on within the individual as well as between individuals who have differing preferences.

INTUITIVE PREFERENCE

Intuition has been called a hunch, the Eureka factor, the flash of insight, a vague feeling and a calm knowing of what had to be done. In Roy Rowan's book *The Intuitive Manager* he explains intuition:

The Eureka factor, that sudden, illuminating, "I've found it" flash, has been referred to again and again by scientists attempting to describe the key element in their discovery process. Most are quick to admit that scientific breakthroughs do not seem to evolve slowly from a sequence of deductions. They spring finally from hunches that cannot be completely explained. "There are no logical paths to these (natural) laws," admitted Albert Einstein. "Only intuition resting on sympathetic understanding of experience can reach them." He called the theory of relativity "the happiest thought of my life." (p. 4)

The intuitive preference indicates a propensity for simultaneously processing information in a total response as opposed to a careful inspection of each of the parts. All managers occasionally use a combination of both sensing and intuiting. Leaders must *consistently* use both.

Let's look at the impact of an intuitive preference. Intuitive types are hooked on possibility and improvement. They naturally resist routine and structured ways of performing tasks. Intuitors look at a situation and immediately begin a process of associating what they are observing with the rich internal database of impressions. They integrate the immediate situation as well as past and future implications. Holistically integrating information frequently causes intuitors to see a situation quite differently from the sensor, who is focusing on the details of what is presently happening. When intuitors scan their own information base and come up with connections and patterns that are unseen in the current situation, sensors can easily conclude that intuitors are making off-the-wall observations.

Sensors look at the situation to see what facts could have spurred such remarks and see nothing to validate such a perspective. They see no transition that would lead them to that viewpoint and thus conclude that the intuitor doesn't know what s/he is talking about. It may be just as difficult for intuitors to understand why sensors don't see the possibilities as it is for sensors to understand the weird observations of intuitors.

Intuitors value inspiration. The energizers of consciousness are those flashes of insight that inspire fresh understanding. Thus, mundane, routine tasks are seen as killers of consciousness by strong intuitors. Routine tasks are done best by intuitors when they have low energy or a float period without concentration. The body performs the routine tasks without too much conscious focus.

Innovation and creativity are natural forms for intuitors. They like to start things. They are initiators, inspirers, innovators. Rarely, however, do you find intuitors who are content. Their continual pursuit of improvement produces a restlessness that is difficult to master. This drive for improvement causes an intensity that can be alarming to sensors. The restless rearrangement of information to maximize possibilities creates what sensors might experience as a vortex of power. The rushing, swirling force to find another way of doing something may drive the intuitor to become oblivious of the facts in the physical surroundings. As the concentration becomes more intense in finding the "new way," the intuitor may take on a messianic zeal that seems threatening to the practical, realistic sensor.

Intuitors are much less likely to compare themselves to other people. They are a bit indifferent to what other people are doing. Rarely do they take their value from the external environment. Intuitors are relatively field independent, meaning they rarely look for validation of insights in external evidence. Intuitors are very independent. They rarely need status objects to compare their success with others. Sensors are more field dependent, meaning they are more dependent upon physical surroundings and comparative models to determine their place in the world.

Intuitors can become so absorbed in achieving a break-through, in putting together a new plan or initiating an enterprise, that they may pay little attention to what is going on around them. The present may fade away in their consciousness, and they become totally absorbed in making the possibility happen.

Charismatic leadership is a possibility if they become focused on an idea that involves their beliefs, innovation, and improvement. They can generate such intensity, such clarity, and such focus that they inspire others with the belief that the impossible is, in fact, possible.

Intuitors can usually blend experience, opportunity, and innovation when they start to focus on a situation. When the intuitive leap occurs, they see old problems in new ways. They access their information base, which contains everything they have ever heard or known that relates to the subject. They relate dissimilar bits of information in a new way, providing connections they may never have seen before. They receive the insight; they do not consciously know the process by which they arrived at the insight. They received the insight without knowing the process of thinking by which it happened. Sensors have intuitive flashes also, but find it very hard to trust a flash that cannot be immediately verified by their senses. Sensors who have learned to develop their trust of their intuition are on their way to information skills required for leadership. Intuitors who have learned to develop their sensory awareness of the physical world are on their way also.

SENSOR AND INTUITOR CHARACTERISTICS

SENSOR	INTUITOR
Practical	Idealistic
Concrete	Abstract
Realistic	Conceptual
Focused on today	Focused on tomorrow
Prefers factual interpretation	Prefers possibility interpretation
Tends to be physically competitive	Tends to be intellectually competitive

Produces steadily	Produces cyclically
Results-oriented	Idea-oriented
Dislikes change	Likes variety and challenge
Sensible	Imaginative
Prefers step-by-step specific routine	Prefers "big picture" — overall or holistic viewpoint
Dislikes ambiguity	Dislikes concretized situations
Dislikes long-range planning	Dislikes too much structure
Prefers concrete examples and facts	Prefers symbols, concepts, and meanings

Sensors derive their greatest satisfaction from today's action, while intuitors are inspired by tomorrow's possibility.

Intuitors frequently provide interesting, fresh ways of looking at a situation, which stimulates others to see differently. They challenge and force people to reexamine their perceptions. They are stimulated by creative problem-solving. Throw them a problem and watch the energy rise. They can make sense out of random data. Especially gifted at seeing patterns, they find order in the disorderly, clarity in chaos. Is there any doubt about our assertion that development of intuitive processing is essential to lead today's organization?

Sensors are usually talented at structured tasks and thinking, while intuitors find their outlet in integrative tasks that require them to find threads of meaning that produce the picture of understanding. Sensors prefer structure and a narrow frame of reference, whereas intuitors prefer possibility thinking and a wide frame of reference.

The general American population has 75% sensors and 25% intuitors. (p. 45, Briggs & McCaulley, 1986) With three out of four people preferring sensing, the norms of society are strongly influenced by sensing values: work hard and play hard (pleasure-lovers), enjoy possessions (consumer-oriented), live as well as the Joneses (status-oriented), compete with the best of them (competition-focused), get what you want (ambitious to succeed), and do what you are supposed to do (accept responsibility). These values do not exclude intuitors, but intuitors are more likely to reject sensor values or find a way to apply their desires for status, pleasure, competition, ambition, and responsibility to ideas, thinking, innovation, and improvement rather than to the finite world.

Intuitors are more difficult to understand than sensors. Intuitive thought processes of the imaginative, integrative mental world are harder to follow than the physical-world, factual processes of sensors. We are not asserting intellectual superiority; we are asserting the greater complexity of the intuitive process. Since intuitors frequently arrive at conclusions without conscious reasoning process, they are more complex.

Sensors usually make a conscious examination of the observed facts in the physical world, while intuitors use lightning-fast integration in the unconscious and receive the result in consciousness. Many times intuitors cannot explain exactly how they arrived at the result; they are just sure of the result of the process. Sensors are usually not as facile in activating their unconscious information base. If the answer appears suddenly in the sensor mind without a map of how the answer arrived, it is likely to be rejected. They can't trust the result if they do not have a sound understanding of its meaning. Intuitive flashes of insight are very quick, while sensing observation of the situation is slower. The intuitive insight can rapidly integrate thousands of bits of data from the unconscious memory base. The sensor insight can integrate conscious observations at a much slower rate with no more than seven bits of data processed simultaneously. The sensor moves toward insight in a step-by-step thinking process, while the intuitor prefers the global approach.

Sensors tend to use habitual decision-making processes; intuitors are more likely to make split-second decisions. When the excitement of the insight inspires the intuitor, the decision may come very quickly.

Intuitors are frequently operating from an internal vision of the possible. They use an intuitive guidance system to steer them toward the target. When they are getting off course or something endangers the vision, a warning system goes off and the attention is immediately directed to the interference. If an intuitor becomes too overwhelmed with fear or anxiety, the guidance system can become so jammed that clarity of the vision is impaired. As a result, intuitors can become overly anxious and blocked when their intuitive guidance system is inaccessible.

Sensors are more likely to set attainable goals and use a methodical plan of systematic work to achieve the goals. They will be more measurable and easier to evaluate than the intuitive vision. Thus, the sensor is usually working on that which is measurable and has a specific target and a payoff that can be measured in "real world" trophies.

SENSOR PROCESSES	INTUITOR PROCESSES
Taking notes	Picturing the meaning
Organizing and outlining	Seeing patterns
Setting priorities	Integrating the big picture
Observing body language	Responding to body language
Analyzing the facts	Feeling the subtle relationships
Comparing and judging	Discovering convergent and divergent points of view
Setting goals and objectives	Finding innovative approaches
Eliminating extraneous parts	Sifting the whole for meaning
Writing	Drawing
Making a list	Using a symbol to picture the idea
Using machines	Arranging ideas, things, or spaces
Looking at the clock	Checking energy level
Shaking hands with someone	Relating to their presence
Separating the parts of a problem and putting them in order	Seeing the relationship between people and the parts of the whole problem
Focus specifically on facts of the situation	Unfocus and get an intuitive feel for the situation
Check the details	Check the meanings, the flavor, the general feel of the situation

CASE STUDY: INTUITOR-SENSOR CONFLICT

In management meetings, we have seen numerous communication breakdowns occur as a result of the intensity of the intuitor and the incredulity of the sensor. The executive director of a large organization called us and asked if we could provide a communication assessment of his top management group. He was agitated as he talked about them. He said:

If I can't get them straightened out, I'm going to get rid of the whole bunch and find me a group of team players who are gutsy, risk-taking thinkers. Every time I try to get them to look at a new idea, they oppose it and tell me it won't work. I'm going to find a group of people who can initiate ideas and make reasonable assessments. I'm sick of their negative attitudes.

I went to the organization to begin interviews and process observation. A pattern began to emerge quickly. Management group members talked about their boss's impulsive embracing of new, untested ideas. They talked about the need to "head him off at the pass," before he went off in an impractical, unworkable direction. They cited incidents where he had begun implementation of an idea before practical considerations could be worked out. They told emotional versions of the disastrous effects of innovative ideas that were started without a structured plan.

The eight-person group had six sensors and two intuitors. Sensor thinking dominated the management meetings. Three of the sensors were highly extroverted and tended to speak often. They tended to resist new ideas and automatically contributed the reasons why the ideas would not work.

As I observed their interactions, I saw a recurring problem. The director would offer an idea, and while he was still experiencing the intuitive high of expressing and exploring the idea, the sensors would interrupt him to begin countering his idea. The director would become angry and red-faced as he battled the "negativity" and fought for his idea. Consequently, the director began to irrationally fight for ideas that were exploratory rather than being courses of action. When he heard the expected "negative opposition" he overreacted by using bluster and force to make them accept the idea. As a result, ideas were being implemented that were reactions to dissent rather than deliberative, desirable actions.

We facilitated a workshop to help them identify the dysfunctional communication interactions. Not only were they seeing information differently, but their sense of timing in the interaction was off. The group was trained to see the nonverbal manifestations of the boss's intuitive high. His face would flush, he got up from the table, drew symbolic representations of his idea on the whiteboard, spoke louder and more enthusiastically when he was in the intuitive rush of idea exploration. That was certainly no time to interrupt him with practical or realistic questions. If a staff member interrupted him during the intuitive high, the boss responded with aggressive rebuke. Five of the management team said little. They chose to keep their ideas to themselves rather than risk the onslaught of wrath. The three that spoke most frequently seemed to get energized by the competitive struggle for idea dominance.

The staff learned to read the boss's signals. When he returned to the table, slowed his delivery, summarized his ideas, relaxed his face, assumed a reflective demeanor, and asked for their best thinking, they could then articulate their concerns, objections, or questions. After giving birth to the idea and assuming a more benign distance from the birthing process, the intuitive boss was now ready to go into the cleaning-up process. He was then ready to look at his idea with a bit more objectivity and expected intensive examination of his idea from his staff. If they missed the timing, however, it caused trouble.

They learned to be more responsible for their styles and more responsible for the effect of their preferences on the group processes. The director was better at communicating when he wanted them to listen and when he wanted their deliberative examination of the possibilities. He began to use their strengths of realistic assessment and realistic implementation procedures. They began to relax and value his ability to see opportunity in chaos and his ability to produce innovative solutions to what had appeared to them as insoluble problems. The two intuitives began to contribute more to discussions, and productivity and teamwork improved.

Jobs have predominately sensor tasks or predominately intuitor tasks. Since all of us have both sensor and intuitor capacities, it is useful to get a more realistic look at the differences.

The situation described below illustrates the thought stream of sensing and intuitive impressions.

Sensor — Factual information		*Intuitive — Impressions and patterns*
WHO	You and your boss	Hassled, disagreeing, nervous
WHAT	Boss wanted Jones to do it	Conflict, difficulty, wrong
WHERE	Boss's office	Sun shining through the windows, Jones has no vision — sees commas instead of concepts. See Jones in mouselike scurry to examine unimportant aspects while the overall work suffers.

WHEN	7:45 A.M.	Boss doesn't usually arrive this early . . . Never calls anyone into his office until after 8:30. This must indicate his concern over your accepting Jones as his choice . . . Boss likes to get things over with if he expects opposition.
WHY	He thinks Jones has more experience in this sort of thing.	Jones has been golfing with the boss . . . showed him a letter of appreciation from a customer. Boss is forgetting Jones has not been able to solve complex problems. He's a good technician but not a visionary.
HOW	He's telling you to accept Jones as project coordinator and help him develop his problem-solving skills.	Jones's nuts-and-bolts approach will send the work group up the wall — they like more freedom.

Sensing is predominately a left-brain process, while intuiting is predominately a right-brain process. The sensor function provides the information input from the physical environment (who, what, when, where, why, how), while the intuitive provides the meaning, integration, impression, and implications of the interaction. Thus we support our argument for development of both processes for leadership. One of the processes will be natural, and the other will require skills development.

SENSOR TASKS	INTUITOR TASKS
Contracting	Composing
Accounting	Counseling
Budgeting	Planning
Bookkeeping	Forecasting
Classifying	Mapping
Compiling	Simplifying
Scheduling	Processing
Reporting	Reacting
Dissecting	Integrating
Speaking	Gathering
Prioritizing	Designing

Reading	Visualizing
Reviewing	Troubleshooting
Editing	Reflecting
Supervising	Decorating

Many tasks require both processes. Driving requires an awareness of details *and* overall traffic conditions. Advertising requires detail *and* strategies. Arranging requires physical moves *and* organizing pattern. Editing requires attention to grammatical structure *and* meaning. Persuading requires factual evidence *and* relationship of premise to argument. Negotiating requires attention to detail *and* anticipation of moves. Collaborating requires give and take, fact and implication. Delegating requires specific delegation with general supervision. Inventing requires a new way of thinking with a physical development of product. Listening requires an integration of observations, facts, impressions, and feelings.

Information is a crucial power source. The way we manage it can increase or decrease our power to produce.

Let's review some of the differences between sensing and intuitive processing.

SENSOR	INTUITOR
Idea tester	Idea generator
Factual	Instinctual
Task-driven	Improvement-driven
Cautiously tests	Intuitively leaps and accepts
Sees details for specific reality . . . physical reality	Scans speedily for general impression
Has pre-programmed viewpoint according to norms and experience	Rejects pre-programmed viewpoint and looks for a new view
Has strong expectations	Has gentle flashes
Prefers to make improvements incrementally	Prefers to make improvements by changing systems, structure, or procedures
Linear	Simultaneous

Sensors and intuitors see the world differently. Both perspectives are essential, whether within you or among you and your co-workers.

CHANGE

Change is coming so rapidly that it is accelerating at exponential rates. Leaders need to assess the current situation clearly (sensing) and respond innovatively (intuiting). To get a clear picture of the rate of change, let's look at Carolyn Corbin's description in her book *Strategies 2000*.

> One-half of the energy consumed in the past 2,000 years has been used in the last 200 years.
>
> One-half of all products on supermarket shelves were not there a decade ago and will likely not be there a decade from now.
>
> For a child who is ten years old today, there will be four times as much knowledge available to that child when he goes to college as is available to him now. When that ten-year-old child becomes fifty years of age, knowledge will have increased thirty-two (32) times today's level.
>
> People who are seventy years of age or older today have seen most of the technological innovaton that has taken place in the United States. It is almost staggering to the mind to believe that most of the people living today have actually seen and experienced a total technological revolution in America. (pp. 25–26)

With that rate of change the intuitive ability to see pattern in chaos, to find a course in uncharted waters, and to bring maximum clarity to bear on a situation is essential. Also essential is the sensing ability to assess accurately the details of the physical situation, see a realistic plan of work, and communicate stable work processes to achieve the goal. A leader must clearly be able to access both sensing and intuiting and also be able to help others develop their skills to achieve balanced perception.

A review of the strengths and weaknesses of each preference is helpful, beginning with sensing.

SENSOR STRENGTHS AND WEAKNESSES

STRENGTH:	Likes observable facts
WEAKNESS:	May overlook implications and meanings

Example: The setting is a midsize bank on the West Coast. Dale, the manager of the credit card section, is an extroverted sensor. He is skilled at observing the specific events occurring around him. Alan is also an extroverted sensor. He has worked for Dale for three months.

Alan was quick to recognize that his boss valued punctuality, a clean desk, careful observance of breaks, and neat appearance. Those values were easy to read, so Alan was meticulous about observing the implied rules. He arrived at his desk precisely ten minutes ahead of start time, and carefully took lunch and coffee breaks so that he was at his desk at the exact moment he was supposed to be. He dressed neatly and was the image of order. His measurable behavior indicated that he was a model employee. His paperwork had the same characteristics of timeliness, neat appearance, and order.

Dale was pleased with what he saw of Alan. He evaluated what his senses told him and concluded that Alan was an excellent employee. He saw nothing to indicate otherwise.

At a workshop on team building, I noticed nonverbal cues of hostility directed toward him from four of his co-workers. As the group participated in team-building exercises, I saw Alan consistently but subtly give tasks away that required hard work. In four projects he traded roles with others until he got the least strenuous task. He was charming and smiling in his trading, but team members were showing more and more nonverbal cues of annoyance with him.

As we started the fifth project, Alan began his pattern of rearranging the assigned workloads. One exasperated co-worker added verbal to her nonverbal messages when she said, "Alan, you can just keep the role you were assigned. It won't hurt you to break a sweat for the team." Dale had been observing the group and seemed quite surprised at the remark.

I then facilitated a discussion about how the workshop exercises showed similar patterns in their regular work group. Slowly, the pattern of Alan's manipulation of the work group became clear. We worked through the dynamic and refocused on the goals of teamwork.

As Dale and I were debriefing the workshop, he remarked, "I was really shocked when Jane got irritated with Alan. I thought she was just jealous of his having it all together. She sounded bitchy. If you hadn't drawn the others out, I would never have picked up their feelings about him. He sure looks like the ideal employee."

When Dale returned to the office, he pulled a sample of Alan's work and found to his disappointment that the content contained a number of careless errors. Dale looked at the neat and orderly form of the reports and assumed accuracy of assessment as well. He failed to notice that Alan put most of his concentration into the image of good work and not enough sweat into doing good work. Dale had inferred that Alan's careful attention to timeliness also implied careful attention to detail.

As he thought more about the situation, he began to recall situations where workers were giving very subtle hints at their dissatisfaction with Alan's unwillingness to do tasks that were challenging or messy. Dale just did not pick up the cues, since his perception gave him evidence of "appropriate employee behavior." He saw selective facts, but missed the impact of the manipulation.

STRENGTH:	Likes information explained step-by-step
WEAKNESS:	May not see the guiding principle behind the information

Example: Tom had been with the company for nineteen years. He had gradually worked into a mid-management position. A new president had been hired and immediately began to decentralize the organization. At a meeting with the department head, Tom was told that he would be managing his own budget now and would be expected to prepare a budget presentation for the following year.

Tom said, "Well, exactly what do you want me to do? I look at what I had this year. Count the increase in workload . . ." Tom stayed on the subject until he had worked out the eleven steps he had to go through to get the budget presentation ready.

Tom went through the steps carefully and prepared his work. He was so intent on getting the figures and paperwork right that he didn't even consider the implied expectations that came with the change. He failed to see that the guiding principle behind the task was an expectation that he assume a more responsible role of decision-making than he had formerly used. His boss told me, "We are expecting our mid-managers to become leaders in their units rather than just bureaucratic passers of information. We are expecting them to become innovative and adept at maximizing profits. The next step is to turn them into individual profit centers."

One might question the integrity of the company's strategy to implement change without clearly laying out their thinking. Part of their strategy was to see which of the managers were sharp enough to see what the change in the budget process meant. The executive team intended to observe the budget presentations carefully in order to identify "fast-track" potential to groom for upper-level management. They were looking for those managers who could receive a task, identify the implications of change, be self-starters in their move to act on the implications, and present a budget that showed an integration of their past roles and future capabilities.

STRENGTH:	Prefers the practical, the realistic, and the present
WEAKNESS:	May reject new, innovative ideas and may not see future demands in time

Example: Oscar was a twenty-four-year-old sensor who scored a 51 on sensing when he took the Myers-Briggs Indicator. He had such a strong preference for sensing that he appeared to be stuck. He completed his accounting degree at twenty-one and passed his CPA test at twenty-four. He liked the practical application of accounting principles.

He worked with an internal audit group of a large oil company. The audit group had a number of audit supervisors who assembled different groups of audit employees for different jobs.

Oscar liked auditing. His approach was to get an assignment in the audit group and painstakingly examine the details until he had traced a clear step-by-step process through designated transactions. His approach was thorough and meticulous — two traits that he knew were important in his profession.

As audit costs were rising, the audit supervisors called a meeting to discuss more cost-effective and efficient strategies to provide a quality audit. They were unequivocal about the quality of the audit. It would remain excellent. Their focus was to search for new ways to perform that quality of work.

They decided to try a thirty-minute team meeting at the beginning of each work day. They would discuss the work of the previous day to integrate their understanding, share insights, and look for clues of where the auditee was performing exceptionally well and where performance problems might exist.

Oscar steadfastly refused to contribute to the discussion at the morning meetings. He sat there and quietly worked on his notes from the day before. Oscar viewed the meetings as a waste of time, though he was careful not to say that verbally. He didn't have to: his behavior was obvious.

On the seventh morning of the team meeting, the discussion paid off. An innocuous clue picked up by one auditor sparked a similar clue found in another part of the company. Within twenty minutes they understood that their original audit plan was not going to produce the most help to the auditee. They excitedly reorganized their strategy and reassigned tasks. Oscar had not been following the information. He was lost. He just wanted to go back and finish the audit task he had been working on. The new information made it unnecessary for him to continue that approach. He became angry and resentful. He did not see the value of changing the strategy.

Oscar was slow to apply himself to his changed assignment. He did not realize that the way of the future audit in the company had just been verbalized. Audit teams in the future would be more flexible and interactive as problem-solvers and information-sharers on a daily basis. No longer would they wait for weekly or monthly integration of their findings. Future demands required the audit team to be quicker, more integrative in their findings, more adaptable, and more able to identify the management practices that were both successful and those that were causing the auditee trouble. They were required by their company to be business consultants — not just accountants declaring integrity of business processes after the fact. They were being asked to help assess future implications of current practices.

STRENGTH:	Prefers the tried and tested
WEAKNESS:	May use obsolete methods or techniques

Example: In the previous example, Oscar clung stubbornly to the audit approach that best suited his sensor style. He was unwilling to change to the current method of using both the sensing (accurate attention to detail) and the intuitive (sharing information to see patterns of performance).

Oscar was so scornful of the team meeting approach for sharing information that he was given the option of transferring to the accounting department or leaving the company. The internal audit group was changing to meet auditee demands; Oscar's unwillingness to change made him inappropriate for the situation.

In this case, his accounting techniques were not obsolete; his preference for a more traditional audit process was no longer the most viable to meet the changing needs of the auditee.

STRENGTH:	Demands proof
WEAKNESS:	May miss opportunities while waiting for proof

Example: A civil service procurement officer scored 61 on sensing preference. He was certain that he had mastered the major chunks of information needed to run the procurement process.

The two-star general in charge of the division had little tolerance for inefficiency or unresolved problems.

In the past two months the procurement officer had received seven complaints about the slow turn-around time in his department. Each time he received a complaint, he dismissed it because he did not see proof that his group had done anything wrong.

At a management group meeting with the general, the disbursing officer and the director of engineering raised the issue of procurement time lags that were causing problems with their suppliers. The general told the procurement officer to look into that issue immediately.

The procurement officer returned to his department and asked his staff to find proof that both the disbursing officer and the director of engineering had been remiss in their interface with procurement. While his staff was preoccupied with proving that the fault was not in their department, a small supplier called to tell him that he still had not received his contract for materials that had been authorized by phone six weeks earlier. The procurement officer angrily asked for verification of the authorizing phone call. The supplier was notably offended.

Each time the procurement officer received messages that something was not functioning smoothly, he demanded proof of the charge. He did not look at the processes within his department, but took the position that others were picking on "my guys." He was directing his staff to defend their positions. He missed the opportunity to review the work processes within his own unit.

When the general said he wanted immediate resolution of the problem, that is just what he meant. He was livid when the offended supplier's senator called and asked what was wrong with procurement.

Ten minutes later, a colonel on the general's staff walked into the procurement office to begin an immediate assessment of work processes. The procurement officer was effectively removed from the decision-making loop while the colonel assessed the problem, made changes in the process, instituted a scheduling procedure, and supervised the changes.

In the private sector, a businessperson who waits for proof that the market is changing may be too late. Competitors may already be ready to grab the market share.

STRENGTH:	Likes to get things done
WEAKNESS:	May cut too many corners, push too hard, and do things too quickly

Example: Sam scored as an ESTJ (extrovert, sensor, thinker, judge) on the Myers-Briggs Indicator. He ran his investment business with a hand of iron. He was accustomed to making quick decisions and ordering people around.

As a successful businessman, he was asked by the chamber of commerce to chair the leadership training program for the city. Forty of the brightest and most promising young leaders in the community were chosen to receive nine months of leadership training. It was an honor to be selected for the program. They ranged in age from twenty-five to thirty-five.

Sam brought the same domineering approach to his chairmanship as he used in his business. The highly intelligent, individualistic group of "baby boomer" leaders-in-training began to rebel against his attempts to run rough-shod over their suggestions. Whenever they questioned, he raised his voice and gave his favorite saying: "Business ain't a democracy. You don't always get a vote."

At the second meeting of the group, the facilitator had asked for some supplies. Sam denied the request with a quick retort: "Let them improvise. We're not running a charm school here. Management is making do with what you have. It would take more time and money than it's worth." When the group arrived and found that they did not have the materials they considered essential for the learning experience, they asked Sam about it.

He angrily responded: "Yours is not to question, but to do."

The battle lines were clearly drawn with that remark. Sam had a number of problems that a sensor may have: too much belief in the hierarchy of roles, unwillingness to notice that things are changing, too much expectation of traditional response to commands. This situation leads directly to the next strength and weakness.

STRENGTH:	Commands others; orders others
WEAKNESS:	May not discuss or ask enough questions or take the time to build group support

Example: Sam's sensor characteristics are rooted in a traditional belief in roles, authority, and hierarchy. He believes rules are rules, and everyone should bow to them.

When the testy group of young leaders questioned his way of managing the program, he responded with cutting statements and assertion of his power and authority. Unfortunately, his responses were just like waving the red flag at the bull. The group coalesced immediately into a singular unit to rebel against his authority. The rest of the year was a battleground — a struggle for power and control. What had begun as a noble program for the development of leadership became a war between authoritarian and participatory approaches to power.

STRENGTH:	Likes competition
WEAKNESS:	May compete over unimportant issues and become driven; may translate non-competitive activities into win-lose situations

Example: Andy is the personnel director of a large civil service department located on a military base. He is an avid competitor. He personally plays an excellent game of golf, tennis, and racquetball. When he came to the personnel department it was a little-known unit that did not have an exceptional record of service. To have no identity was unthinkable to Andy.

He immediately reorganized the work groups. His first objective was to get recognition for the Personnel Department. He canvassed the sports talent among the group and immediately got them enrolled in base competition. The especially articulate staff were ordered to volunteer for committees and to make skilled presentations with professional charts and view graphs. He laid out a public relations strategy that would have impressed the best. His goal was to get the department reputation established.

In addition to ordering the staff to become instantly involved in competing outside the department, he set up numerous in-house competitions. He compared the work done in one office to that of another, urging the least favored one to get with the program. He used terms with his staff such as, "Don't let Ted get ahead of you. He turned in three reports yesterday"; "She beat you to work this morning by five minutes"; "Hey, you are the best dressed person in the office today. The rest of you better get with it." Andy became so focused on competition, that he forgot that the original purpose of a personnel office is service.

He drove a red Z-28, joined an exclusive country club, and wore tailored suits. None of these would constitute a problem if not combined with his absorption with competition.

His staff talked about being driven day and night. They even joked about keeping score on most cups of coffee drunk or not drunk, most trips to the bathroom, and fewest noticeable grimaces at management meetings.

Andy had clearly lost his perspective.

Most of the examples used here demonstrate how a strength can easily become a weakness when not properly balanced. Leaders must keep the balance within their strongest preference as well as between the two kinds of perception. Let's review the sensor strengths and weaknesses:

Sensor

STRENGTHS	WEAKNESSES
Likes observable facts	May overlook implications and meanings
Likes information explained step-by-step	May not see the guiding principle behind the information
Prefers the practical, the realistic, and the present	May reject new, innovative ideas and may not see future demands in time
Prefers the tried and tested	May use obsolete methods or techniques
Demands proof	May miss opportunities while waiting for proof

Likes to get things done	May cut too many corners, push too hard, and do things too quickly
Commands others; orders others	May not discuss or ask enough questions or take the time to build group support
Likes competition	May compete over unimportant issues and become driven; may translate noncompetitive activities into win-lose situations

INTUITOR STRENGTHS AND WEAKNESSES

STRENGTH:	Thinks quickly; reads between the lines
WEAKNESS:	May skim information and miss essential variables and omit facts

Example: A data processing director in a large savings and loan association was having communication problems. His boss asked us to work with him. The Myers-Briggs revealed a style preference of ENTJ (extrovert, intuitor, thinker, judge). He scored 37 as an intuitor. Talking with him showed that he was an undisciplined intuitor. He talked in generalities and paid little attention to specifics.

We attended a management meeting between he and his boss. The sensor boss was quite methodical in discussing issues. The intuitive data processing director found it difficult to stay interested in what the boss was saying. During the interaction the boss asked him to do six specific things. After the second request was made, the intuitor became involved in the possibilities. He barely seemed to listen during the rest of the interaction. He appeared to be preoccupied. The intuitor referred back to the second request three times — a good indication that he was skimming the present conversation and was taking internal flights of fancy stimulated by his interest in the second request.

The sensor boss had notes about the six requests and the deadlines set for each. When we returned to the intuitor's office, I asked him which of the six specific things he was going to do first. He looked at me a bit puzzled. "What six things? I only remember three." He was skimming over the discussion which bored him; his mind moved on to things of greater interest. He had taken no notes and returned to his office unable to recall the specific deadlines set by his boss. That was exactly the type of behavior that had made the boss call us.

We worked with the intuitor to help him develop the mental discipline to develop his sensor focus and attention to detail. He had to discipline his mind. He had to consciously learn to control his attention. To hold it in the physical world of detail was not as energizing for him as to let it roam freely in the intuitive process of possibility.

STRENGTH:	Uses "big picture" thinking while synthesizing random data
WEAKNESS:	May leave things dangling, use too many topics, and be scattered and unfocused

Example: "Big picture" thinking could be described as seeing a theme in not yet understandable chaos. It is an overall intuitive impression of the organizing principle of the multiple data in the chaotic situation. "Big picture" thinking is the ability to see what the randomness indicates, predicting where things are and where they are headed.

An intuitive CEO gave an opening speech at the business planning retreat of the executive staff. He knew that the company had a rough year ahead. Profit margins were narrowing, competition was intense, union negotiations were coming up, and many departments were working long hours. He organized his remarks with a brief outline. As he thought about what he wanted to say, he became internally engrossed with the symbol of a soaring eagle. The more he thought about his company and the problems, the more he envisioned his company soaring above the competition like the eagle. He got excited about the imagery and began to see all kinds of applications of the symbol.

He appeared before his largely sensor executive team. The principle sensors were the heads of finance, engineering, operations, maintenance, and purchasing. The CEO began to talk about the challenges involved in the coming year. He laced together an intricate picture of the principles of economics, world trade, the dollar strength, market trends, management practices, and finished with his grand challenge.

"Our job, gentlemen, is to soar above our competition like the majestic eagle. We will fly higher, faster, and further than any of them can reach. We will set our goal to be 28% better than the competition. We will be the eagle among sparrows. Now let's get to work and develop the most innovative business plan ever."

As he became more and more inspired by the symbols and images, he was lost inside his own experience. He failed to notice the subtle exchange of nonverbal looks of alarm. He lost the ability to notice what was happening in the physical world around him. He was inspiring himself in a dandy way. Unfortunately, most of his staff were not soaring with him.

His executive staff had wanted him to set a clear, measurable course for the challenging year ahead. They were confused and unclear just how to apply the eagle story to the reality of finding a way to be 28% better than the competition.

As they took a coffee break before moving into their work groups to begin the nitty-gritty job of updating their business plan, the finance executive remarked to the engineer, "I wonder if the CEO looked closely at what his eagle is going to do to the poor sparrows who work under that lofty 28% load he just placed on them. He's got to be crazy if he thinks we can get 28% more productivity out of an already worn-out work force."

The maintenance director retorted, "Hey, John, I think he was looking at you when he talked about the national debt. That's your assignment for next year."

The CEO had misread his staff. He left their real questions unanswered, introduced too many topics, and used symbols that they did not relate to as a meaningful way to get them focused on the task at hand.

STRENGTH:	Conceptualizes easily, sees possibilities, and recognizes patterns
WEAKNESS:	May overrate possibilities and see secondary instead of primary patterns

Example: An intuitive CEO needed to select a new chief operating officer (COO). The retiring COO was a personable, hard charger who scored as an ESTJ (extrovert, sensor, thinker, judge) on the Myers-Briggs. He was friendly and managed by wandering around. He was well liked and set a relaxed tone at the office.

The CEO looked at the challenges ahead and decided that he wanted to fill the position with a COO who had fifteen years of operations management in a business climate similar to theirs. The CEO thought the main hiring issue was to find someone with credible experience. His recognition of the popularity of the retiring COO guided his choice of experience as the main control variable in hiring.

We discussed the hiring challenge. I saw a number of variables: 1) replacing a charismatic COO raised a transition issue; 2) the former COO was strong with people but a bit careless with internal controls; 3) he was a persuasive debater who served as an excellent reality tester for the CEO; 4) the retiring COO was working closely with the management readiness group and was the mentor for seven of the brightest; 5) he was popular and tough; 6) his replacement would have a challenging position to fill; 7) the retiring COO was quite popular in the community.

From those and other variables, the CEO felt most strongly that depth of experience was the critical variable. As it turned out, the replacement was an ISTJ (introvert, sensor, thinker, judge) who was brilliant and hard-working. Unfortunately, he had never developed his extroverted, intuitive skills. He had eighteen years of operational experience, was a brilliant man, and came from a reputable company. However, he had little understanding of the interpersonal relationship expectations of the job.

The ISTJ went to his office and stayed for the next six months, working twelve- to fourteen-hour days reading paperwork and mastering the internal systems. During that six months the people dynamic worsened. The seven young employees mentored by the former COO became merciless critics. People complained that they never saw the boss; he was judged harshly for never eating in the company dining room, etc. The main communication they had with the new COO was a barrage of memos and handwritten notes on paperwork they turned in. The new COO was a strong internal audit person.

The CEO's underassessment of the hiring problem was further exacerbated by his failure to supervise the new COO's entry into the organization. The former COO was such a people person that the CEO did not see clearly the different styles. He let the situation go too long before he noticed what was happening.

The intuitive CEO had chosen a secondary variable both for hiring and for integrating the new COO into the organization. As a result, much people energy was lost in frustration and the work in the organization suffered.

| STRENGTH: | Is visionary and individualistic |
| WEAKNESS: | May be impractical, too independent, and ego-centered |

Example: A colonel in the armed services scored as an INTJ (introvert, intuitor, thinker, judge) on the Myers-Briggs Indicator. He is intelligent, tough, and innovative. His military training exposed him to some of the best training and experience to keep his fertile mind expanding.

His work at the war college further expanded his vision of leadership. He saw leadership as someone who is sharp, self-motivated, independent, creative, risk-taking, and right most of the time. In short, he saw himself as the epitome of leadership and looked for others who were like him.

Since the colonel was inspired by ideas, symbols, and images he mistakenly thought everyone else should be. He forgot or did not consciously value the fact that 75% of Americans are sensors, not intuitors. He projected high expectations and expected others to sweat blood in trying to reach them.

He set tough standards and showed little mercy when people continually failed to meet them. He was so independent that he saw his job as setting high standards. The standards, together with his own superb modeling, should be enough to develop people. He did not take the time to see that there is far more to developing people than setting a model to which the majority of them did not relate.

He was so individualistic he never took the time to learn how to develop teamwork. Instead, he tried to order teamwork, which can't be done. Teamwork is a set of attitudes and behaviors that people *give.* Teamwork is not something one can *take* from the work force with an order.

The colonel was a fine specimen of a somewhat closed system. He was physically fit and mentally sharp, but so out of touch with other people that little meaningful communication or modeling occurred. I never met anyone who wanted to be like him.

| STRENGTH: | Works in bursts of energy with good productivity |
| WEAKNESS: | Finds routine tasks tedious and gets bored easily |

Example: When the intuitor is on an "intuitive roll" where everything is coming up sevens, s/he can work on multiple projects at once. While working on one thing, an intuitive flash gives insight on something else and suddenly the intuitor is tossing multiple ideas in the air. When the intuitive burst of energy is in force, the intuitor's productivity is amazing to see. When that energy starts to wane, it is harder to be clear, harder to be creative, harder to focus.

Routine tasks usually bore the intuitor. Many times the intuitor will change the routine just to avoid boredom. I have seen intuitive managers change a standard operating procedure principally due to mental boredom with the old one.

Not only are intuitors intolerant with routine tasks, they are equally intolerant with routine people. Once they know how to read a person's patterns, they tend to become bored unless that person shows more spontaneity of thought or behavior. The intuitor sees boredom as the enemy. Continually focused on improvement and growth, the intuitor wants to wring maximum idea or process stimulation from events, people, or ideas.

STRENGTH:	Develops systems for achieving work
WEAKNESS:	Unrealistic about time required to do the work

Example: A newly appointed regional director in a state-managed federal program replaced an ESFJ (extrovert, sensor, feeler, judge). The new director is an ENTJ (extrovert, intuitor, thinker, judge).

The ESFJ was a stickler for orderly paperwork. She also approached her management job as an extension of her family. She mothered the supervisors who worked for her. She was kind and supportive. She had difficulty reprimanding people. Her main tools were appealing to their goodness and projecting guilt if they brought up unpleasant issues. It was hard for her to confront problems, so she tried to keep the "children" in line by praising cooperative behavior and using innuendos that cause guilt in those who upset her.

The ENTJ took over the position and decided to make sweeping changes. Remember: a sensor is likely to make incremental changes, where an intuitor is more likely to make sweeping system changes. Sensors usually resist change, while intuitors are usually instigators of change.

The intuitor spent the first six weeks interviewing staff and visiting offices and service delivery locations. She studied the situation carefully, looking for overall patterns that indicated dysfunction. At the end of six weeks she announced her reorganization plan. She reassigned people, rearranged geographic districts, changed procedures, altered management meeting times and foremats, and generally introduced systems that matched with her internal vision of the way things should be. She mathematically figured how long she thought each worker should spend with a client. In her time figures, she didn't figure time for late clients, bathroom breaks, intervening phone calls, paperwork, crises, office work, etc. She looked at task and minimum time on task and set the schedule accordingly. Consequently, morale nosedived.

A number of things were overlooked in the ENTJ's approach. She underestimated the amount of time it took to put new systems in place. She underestimated the depth of the employees' feelings. They didn't like her consistent message that what they had been doing had no quality and that she was there to save the day. She gave such general directions that people frequently left the meeting uncertain about what to do next. When people tried to pin her down, she became irritated. She expressed irritation with those who could not think for themselves. She interpreted those who ask for more information as those not intelligent enough to take the general directions and come up with their own specifics.

In her opposition to a mothering approach to management, she refused to supervise the transition. She said, "I want them to think for themselves. I want them to grow, expand, and gain confidence. I want them to manage their units with pride and innovation." In short, she wanted them to manage the way she likes to manage. She wanted to change both the organizational systems and people systems simultaneously.

Intuitor

STRENGTHS	WEAKNESSES
Thinks quickly; reads between the lines	May skim information and miss essential variables and omit facts
Uses "big picture" thinking while synthesizing random data	May leave things dangling, use too many topics, and be scattered and unfocused

Conceptualizes easily, sees possibilities, and recognizes patterns	May overrate possibilities and see secondary instead of primary patterns
Is visionary and individualistic	May be impractical, too independent, and ego-centered
Works in bursts of energy with good productivity	Finds routine tasks tedious and gets bored easily
Develops systems for achieving work	Unrealistic about time required to do the work

BALANCED PERCEPTION

Both sensing and intuiting are critical to survival in today's fast-paced world. We are facing new challenges today for which there is no analog in the past. We must, however, retain a moral, ethical, and value base that helps to sustain the human system while going through great changes.

Our sensing perception is essential for seeing objective facts. It gives us tangible reality. Sensing gives us current sensations of an object; it stimulates our sensory response to external stimuli. Well-developed sensing allows us to be uniquely aware of what is going on around us. It gives us the strongest sensations; allows us to feel, touch, taste, and know through sensory stimuli the sensations of a situation or event. Sensing perception is our mechanism for reading the present, for reacting now, for responding to the moment. It is our principal reality tester. It gives us our physical reality of the situation. A leader cannot afford to have an undeveloped sensing perceptual system.

Our intuitive perception focuses on the future and unrealized possibilities. It allows us to use fresh thinking and slough off group thought, traditional ways, approved methods, and accepted practices. It allows us to see old problems in new ways. Our intuition allows us to see several moves ahead, predict the direction things are going, see the implication of the direction, and prepare to lead the invasion. Intuition allows us to unfocus on today's reality so we can expand, soar, relax, create, or survive. Intuitive perception allows us to scan a situation to get a quick impression. It provides instinctive responses that might save our lives or avoid a disastrous move. It provides us a warning that something is wrong before we have the time to find the evidence in the voluminous stacks of raw data and statistical stacks. Intuition allows us to scan a broad base of unrelated experiences, facts, and understandings and bring them into crisp, clear focus. It offers the release of insight, and the relief of knowing.

An example of need for both sensing and intuiting involves a CPA for an independent oil company. She is an ISTJ (introvert, sensor, thinker, judge). Her accounting background reinforced her sensing and thinking orientation. She was suspicious of intuitive urges. "They are always so vague that I ignore them. I can't tell if it is just anxiety or something real." Notice her inference that anxiety is not real. Remember: the sensor test for reality is testing by the five body senses.

In a discussion with her, she openly ridiculed intuition, calling it that "weird, seance" stuff. I asked her to consider the possibility that intuition was a useful partner to her sensor-thinker approach. Notice I asked her to consider a possibility (intuitor language). She resisted the idea at first and then began to examine the idea. With a flash of insight, via her intuition, she responded with surprise. "Hey, maybe that explains a peculiar habit I have. I've never told anyone this . . . but . . . when I finish an audit, I don't like to let go of it the day I finish it. I go back over it carefully that night looking for errors. I sleep on it . . . then, the next morning, if there's an error, I know it. I've been ashamed to tell anyone. It sounds so crazy."

She discounted her intuition so much that she was embarrassed by her "strange" habit of holding the report overnight. She saw the urge to hold it as nonrational and therefore wrong. She had all of the information in her head. As she relaxed her intellectual control of her dominant left brain processes in sleep, her intuitive processes could scan the thousands of bits of data that went into the report, see the whole picture, and discern major errors.

Conrad Hilton was asked about his successful track record of wise and financially profitable decisions. He said, "You do all you can — thinking, figuring, planning — then you *listen* for a response. I know when I have a problem and have done all I can do to figure it out, I keep listening in a sort of silence 'til something clicks and I feel a right answer." (p. 67, *Executive ESP* by Dean & Mihalasky)

STRATEGY FOR DEVELOPMENT

[Remember: The type of perception you prefer feels more natural and is easier to use. Your natural preference does not require as much energy as your learned perception. One type of perception is natural to you and you must develop the skills of the other type.]

Intuitors are naturally attuned to perceptual, spatial, creative, inventive, integrative, and symbolic thinking. They have difficulty with sensing, categorizing, naming, and observing details. They have to learn skills for those sensing processes that aren't as natural.

Sensors are naturally attuned to observation, action, enjoyment, reality-testing, organizing, sequencing, structuring, and deliberating. They have difficulty with integrating, abstracting, conceptualizing, visualizing, and finding relational connections. They have to learn skills for those intuiting processes that don't come as natural.

Sensors strive to experience the fullest measure of actuality, since this is what gives life its fullest sensations and the greatest enjoyment. Intuitors strive for new insights and situations that give the greatest intensity and therefore release extraordinary enthusiasm. Stable situations can stifle the intuitor, while change can fragment the sensor.

Potential Problems for the Sensor

1. May try to move too quickly to fix something; may patch it up rather than resolve it.
2. May be too direct and harsh, thereby failing to get the information needed for the fullest understanding.
3. May be so certain of the way things *should* be that s/he doesn't take the time to learn what others truly think.
4. May cut corners just to get a task finished; may take risky shortcuts which endanger the long-range quality.
5. May be so certain how people should be, that s/he sounds arrogant and "knows it all."
6. May give too many orders and use too much one-way communication, when discussion might be more appropriate.
7. May not see the implications of actions.
8. May not see the pattern in unrelated or unsequenced events.

9. May get too hooked on enjoyment — or too hooked on hard work and long hours.
10. Under stress, may run over other people's rights, become cold, insensitive, pushy, and domineering.

Potential Problems for the Intuitor

1. May be so out of touch with reality to miss what is going on.
2. May be so abstract that it is difficult to communicate with people.
3. May be so busy with own thoughts to not hear, see, or interpret what is going on.
4. May pick a thought from a conversation and internally make a series of intuitive leaps that are almost impossible for others to follow.
5. May fail to give other people transitions to link ideas, hopping from topic to topic. Experiencing or seeing the information internally, s/he may forget that others need verbal pictures painted.
6. May expend much enthusiasm in developing the idea but have little interest in implementing it; may be great at inventing the "what" and terrible at articulating the "how."
7. May be so disorderly in verbalization that people cannot follow a thought, since thoughts are left dangling as a flight of fancy is taken on another idea.
8. May be so independent and confident to not allow others to join in, trust, or get close.
9. May be so impatient with routine and mundane thinking that s/he becomes harsh, judgmental, and rude.
10. Under stress, may become intolerant, uncompromising, impractical, unrealistic, and dogmatic.

Sensor Developing Intuitive Awareness

The sensor feels more natural reading sensory stimuli from objects, people, and events in the external world; therefore, without conscious work on intuitive perception, the sensor may be much less able to read stimuli from the internal world of ideas, impressions, feelings, and patterns.

The sensor has to learn to focus attention inward. The internal focus produces sensory stimuli also, but it is often more gentle, less demanding, more vague than easily definable external stimuli.

Imagine that you are focusing on a lamp near you. With little effort you can see its shape, color, design, and can use that data to determine if you like, dislike, or feel neutral toward it. Now, focus inside and let your mind produce associations that the lamp evokes. Relax, and let your mind explore and play with the image of the lamp. If you find it easy to unfocus your attention from the external lamp and follow the associations and impressions it evokes, you probably have learned how to switch from sensory attending to intuitive processing. If you try to focus internally and your mind is blocked with the physical reality of the lamp, then you are having difficulty accessing your intuitive processing on demand.

Think of an employee. Do factual details come quickly into mind, or do you feel what it's like to work with that person? Do you focus on face, size, and other details as you get sensory data, or are you seeing a wider scope? Do you instead see the image of the person, know the struggles you've shared, remember the goals s/he is trying to reach?

Listen to the internal sensory impressions — the feelings, the impressions, the overall positive or negative tug. Sensors have to learn to consciously process the internal intuitive signals. The tug in your chest and stomach may be an intuitive warning. The internal intuitive processing is programmed to use body, feelings, and mind when you need a warning for your safety. Internal systems work together to protect you and send you signals of potential danger. If we have our conscious attention locked onto external sensory stimuli, the intuitive process may have difficulty breaking in to get our attention.

Sensors can learn to listen to the more subtle messages of the intuitive process. Leaders will find it impossible to rely only on what they can personally see. They must rely on their intuitive sense to make sense out of vague bits and pieces. They must develop a more pervasive way of scanning information with conscious awareness of subtle warnings to alert them when something is not harmonious with the goal.

Sensors might practice strengthening their conscious awareness of intuitive messages by trying some of the following practices:

1. Learn to get quiet and focus internally.
2. Practice deep breathing as a method of slowing down, relaxing, and looking internally.
3. Select an external sensory object, close your eyes, and let your

intuitive mind play with the object. Don't control or judge — let the intuitive mind expand, flow, and invent ways of looking at the object.

4. Observe several people in a room. Consciously see the pattern in which they are standing. See the objects in the room as colors only, or in hues ranging from light to dark, or in terms of tall or short.

5. Unfocus attention to the details of a situation and see what it reminds you of. Let the mind produce some associations, some patterns.

6. Sensors tend to see what people are doing now. Use an exercise in which you imagine them in the same room five years from now. At first sensors may feel silly stretching the mind in such a way. Remember: the sensing perception is an actuality process and the intuitive perception is a more flexible possibility process.

Sensors can learn to trust their intuitive process as they become more aware of just how it works. The intuitive process can take over in times of crisis where your life is threatened, but the more commonplace use of your intuitive process is helping you to see ahead. The sensor mainly uses conscious attention to see the external world, analyze it, and act on it. Balance would mean that the sensor uses the intuitive process to integrate the internal and external world in a more unfocused, expanding, and relaxing way. Intuition puts things together; sensing takes them apart. There is a time to free the intuition of analytical control and let it play with the information; and there is a time to turn the information over to the sensor for the reality test and implementation. That frees the intuitive process to scan ahead and look for implications that might cause changes right now to avoid the problems ahead.

It takes more energy for sensors to see patterns and possibilities. It takes more energy for intuitors to see concrete reality. Sensors tend to see a situation as permanent. Intuitors look at the same situation and see new possibilities. Sensors like to do things and intuitors like to find meaning in things. Both processes are important.

Intuitor Developing Sensory Awareness

Intuitors are more keenly attuned to their internal world of impressions, ideas, symbols, and images. They may be oblivious to the external world. The internal world is their more natural habitat; thus, for development, they need to develop sensory awareness of the external environment.

Sensors take the direct approach and intuitors tend to take the indirect approach. The sensor can appear too brusque; the intuitor, too scattered. Learning to focus both sensing and intuiting simultaneously is the goal.

Intuitors are usually unrealistic about time. Since time is possibility, then there is always time for one more thing. Intuitors frequently overcommit themselves and underevaluate the amount of time tasks require.

Exercises for Balance

Intuitors can develop greater sensory awareness by consciously exercising external focus. The following exercises might give you an idea of where to start.

1. Select a room in your house or office. Discipline yourself to look at each object in the room. You will probably notice yourself quickly start to scan and cluster things together. Slow down and discipline yourself to really see each object. Notice consciously the shapes, colors, textures, configurations. Make yourself attend to detail. You may discover just how addicted you are to the intuitive scan, particularly if you scored 15 or higher on the Myers-Briggs.
2. Eat a piece of fruit, forcing yourself to keep your conscious attention on the fruit until you have eaten it all. Intuitors get bored quickly and can eat food with little conscious awareness of the flavors and textures beyond the first few bites. The attention wanders from the details of sensory stimuli unless there is an unusual reason to keep it focused. Otherwise, the mind moves on to some internal impression that is more interesting.
3. Think about a person. Go deeper than the flood of impressions and feelings until you begin to see or recall specific details about that person.
4. Focus on some work you are doing. See it as it is, right at this moment. Stop yourself from racing ahead to how to change it or improve it. See it now.
5. Think up some exercises that will give you practice in focusing on the present — exercises for "now" awareness. See if you

can discipline your mind for fifteen minutes with "now" awareness, rather than letting it race on into tomorrow, next week, or next year. See if you can tune in right now.

6. Focus on a situation in which you are involved that dissatisfies you. See if you can go for three minutes of full acceptance without letting your mind refocus, rearrange, or redirect it.

7. See if you can turn off the internal noise, relax, breathe deeply, and go beyond mental activity to internal stillness.

Intuitive and sensory perception operate differently. To access our full potential, we must maximize what is natural and develop excellent skills for what isn't, if we are interested in making the commitment to develop leadership.

— 5 —

Judgment:
Thinker-Feeler

Change affects all dimensions but has a particularly observable effect on the thinking-feeling preference. A strong thinker preference usually has a pattern of analyzing with the head at the time of crisis, while strong feeler preference usually reacts with the heart first.

We frequently have concerned clients who feel defensive about their scores on the thinking-feeling dimension. Those who score high on feeling tend to leap to the conclusion that they don't think. Alternately, high-scoring thinkers assume their score means they have no feelings. We carefully explain that this dimension is a decision preference. Both thinkers and feelers reach decision-point through a reasoning process. The major difference is the way they value evidence in developing their rationale for decisions. The thinker prefers evidence of provable cause-and-effect relationships. The feeler prefers evidence relating to people and personal values. The feeler prefers people and personal values first and then cause-and-effect relationships second. The thinker reverses that order. The preference indicates which is used first — the head or the heart. It's a matter of priorities. Thinker uses head first and then heart. Feeler uses heart first and then head.

THINKER HEAD AND FEELER HEART

The strong thinker sees more validity in rules, situational variables, and possibilities of precedence-setting implications. Thinkers may also plug the people factors into the rational frame, but are not as likely to allow the people factors to alter their decision significantly.

Feelers tend to look at the rules, the variables, but weigh carefully the way people will react to the decision. They are more likely to make a decision that allows extenuating circumstances to alter the rule.

Thinkers tend to be more comfortable with analytically sound decisions based upon cause-effect evidence. Feelers tend to make decisions using right-wrong, good-bad premises. Feelers' decisions are usually strongly influenced by personal values; thinkers' decisions are usually based upon what they perceive to be impersonal logical rationale.

Thinker preference is a male stereotype and feeler preference is a female stereotype. The mental pattern of stereotype predicts that men should be thinkers and women should be feelers. In the general American public, 65% of women score as feelers and 60% of men score as thinkers. These statistics tend to support the stereotypes.

We found different representations in our managerial data base. In our management work with over 12,000 managers, we found 83% of the male managers scored as thinkers and 85% of the female managers scored as thinkers. Our work includes a wide variety of managers from the following areas: banks, savings and loans, military, civil service, state, county, city, criminal justice, hospitals, law firms, CPA firms, social service agencies, companies, and corporations.

Our data indicate that thinker preference dominates the managerial world. When you review typical descriptors of the thinker preference, you find the following: rational, cool under pressure, consistent, questioning, and objective. When you review management literature, you find many of the same words and implications. Only recently have we been bombarded with the publicized need for American managers to be more responsive to workers, customers, and clients.

Management is going to have to come to grips with feelers. The Myers-Briggs data base for general American population shows 65% of women as feelers. Add to that variable the Hudson Institute calculation of new workers entering the work force between 1985 and 2000. Their data indicate 64% will be women. We have statistical reason alone to deepen our understanding of the feeler and thinker preference as a useful foundation for understanding managerial change.

A clearer understanding of feeler judgment and the dynamics that affect it is an essential skill. If you are a feeler, you have a natural inclination to use that process. If you are a thinker, you will have to develop skills in that area.

UNDERREPRESENTATION OF FEELERS IN MANAGEMENT

Why have feelers not been welcomed in large numbers into the managerial ranks? The inference that feelers are not competent managers needs to be reexamined. Are feelers incapable of managing, or does their exclusion in large numbers indicate typical thinker discomfort with the expression of feelings?

Let's look at some of the typical reasoning thinkers use.

1. *Feelers get so emotionally involved — how could they be objective?*
   Thinker implies that emotional involvement precludes objectivity, which leads to further inference that the thinker can be objective by ignoring emotional content of situations. We propose that a problem-solving equation that does not seriously use thorough assessment of sensing, thinking, feeling, and intuiting cannot be objective. We submit that effective problem-solving includes:

   clear sensory assessment of the current situation;

   identification of the main variables developed into a clear, analytical rationale;

   clear feeling assessment of the people dynamics;

   and an aerial view of the way the facts, logic, and feelings fit together.

2. *Feelers are easy to manipulate, and that means trouble in management.*
   Thinker implies that being manipulated through feelings is more dangerous than being manipulated through faulty logic and slanted statistics. We propose that emotional manipula-

tion is easier to spot than intellectualism and logician manipulation.

3. *Feelers get their personal values involved and don't see the situation clearly.* Thinkers imply that feelers' personal values are involved and theirs aren't. We propose that feelers' personal values about people and their rights are easier to spot than thinkers' values of criteria, principles, policy, and laws. Both have values: thinkers see their values as superior to feeler values.

Before you decide that we suggest feeling as a criteria for filling the managerial pool, look clearly at the basic premise of this book. Genuine, long-term leadership requires balance and excellent type development on all four dimensions.

We ask that you reconsider the prejudice of American management toward feelings. Feelings can indeed obscure clear thought; however, we are going further to assert that clear thought implies that feelings have been accurately accounted for in the rationale. We don't mean some distant analysis of feelings, but an actual integration of the real feeling situation into the rationale.

NEED FOR THINKER-FEELER BALANCE

A general in the armed services and I were discussing the need for a balanced thinker-feeler approach. He had thirty years of experience in the military. His ideas of leadership were fashioned from both his peacetime and wartime experiences. He fought in World War II as a teenager, and as an adult in Korea and in Vietnam.

He talked about his earlier ideas about leadership which correspond with the typical description of thinker. Then he became aware that something beyond the authority of the system and logical application of strategy was needed. He talked about the process of becoming aware that *esprit de corps* could not be ordered. It was a happening, a bonding that involved hearts, minds, and bodies.

The general spoke clearly about his feelings of vulnerability and his doubts about his own professionalism as a military officer when he internally realized that feelings were an essential part of real teamwork. He talked about the need for genuine relationships that included knowing what both he and the troops were feeling.

He talked about the need to accept those feelings and not try to rationalize them away. He trusted the clarity that came by accepting those feelings without giving in to them. Recognizing that feelings were not the whole truth of the situation released him to do what he had to do. He summarized his remarks with a phrase that is commonly understood in the military: "There ain't no assholes in foxholes."

We explored the role that feeling awareness plays in correctly assessing a situation. Those who are afraid of feelings can easily misread the whole situation. The general spoke about the risk involved in taking down the analytical shield to get a more clear feel of the situation. He talked about the danger of getting so overwhelmed by his feelings that he could not think clearly. He remembered the precise moment when he discovered that he could be shaking inside with feelings and still think clearly. It was one of the peak experiences of his life — the moment he began to learn about real leadership.

Sometimes, when I am observing a management meeting, I am reminded of a "Star Trek" scene. When an unknown but hostile appearing force approached the *Enterprise,* a command was given: "Force shields up!" I think that is an appropriate picture of a thinker with an undeveloped sense of feeler judgment. The moment a person approaches us with "too much emotion," our analytical force-field goes up to distance us from the uncomfortable and perhaps unknown dynamics of feelings. One young manager could actually feel it happening.

He became aware of the feeling of a shield going up in repeated discussions with his wife. He then began to recognize the same thing happening at work. When his wife was talking to him about an impersonal issue, he was comfortable. The moment she focused on him and demanded to know what he was feeling, his force-field went up. He said, "I can feel it happening. When she expects me to express my feelings, it feels like a wall goes up quickly. I guess it's like a bullet-proof window that moves up from my waist, covering my chest and going all the way to the top of my head. After that window goes up, I usually feel numb behind it. I see myself wanting to give her what she wants, but I can't."

The manager talked about similar experiences he has at work. When an employee projects a need for approval or is too upset when talking, the window goes up. He describes some process of just pulling away from the emotional content of the happening and waiting it out behind the shield. Before you write him off as neurotic, look again.

The manager was raised in an intellectually focused home where reasoned discourse was rewarded and any display of emotion was seen as evidence of weakness. He was a lawyer by profession and a thinker by personality preference. His early value-shaping family experience, combined with his training as a logician and his thinker preference, overdeveloped his natural tendencies and left his emotional development to survive if it could.

Management training in America is primarily geared to reinforce and develop thinker preference. We assert that one cannot sustain a leadership position without development of both thinker and feeler characteristics. One significant way to measure leadership is to look at the growth and development of the followers.

With thinker-feeler in balance, a leader rises above emotional manipulation without blocking emotion-laden information. A leader rises above analytical and intellectual manipulation without blocking the information content. The leader must confront the fear of becoming emotionally overwhelmed or of being intellectually distanced.

THINKER-FEELER DISTRUST

Let's look at some of the behaviors that cause thinkers and feelers to distrust each other.

Thinkers who have not developed feeling awareness in their judgment process have the following characteristics:

Critical	Insensitive
Skeptical	Judgmental
Cold	

Feelers who have not developed thinker awareness in their judgment process have the following characteristics:

Confused	Overly sensitive
Gullible	Unpredictable
Moody	

Someone who has developed both thinker and feeler awareness in the judgment process has the following characteristics:

> Shows validity and compassion
> Demonstrates evaluation and appreciation
> Blends principles and values
> Is open to thoughts and feelings
> Accepts responsibility for both thoughts and feelings
> Objectively weighs both thoughts and feelings

Thinkers like logical analysis, objective and impersonal criteria to draw clean analytical cause-and-effect relationships. Subjectivity and people issues muddy up the cleanness of the equation. Thus, thinkers have a natural tendency to distance themselves from personal aspects of the situation.

Feelers like harmony, acceptance, and compassion. They tend to see objectivity as cold analysis, devoid of sensitive awareness of the impact of the situation. One feeler said, "Thinkers don't consider the emotional effects of their decisions when implemented. How can they be so blind?" Another feeler said, "Why can't thinkers use their logic and reason to arrive at a decision that is both sound and sensitive?"

In many managerial workshops, I have asked groups of thinkers to identify the ways in which feelers hurt their feelings. At first there is loud laughter in the room. Feelers tend to think that I am joking. I also ask feelers to identify the ways thinkers hurt their feelings. That part of the assignment seems more acceptable to both thinkers and feelers.

That workshop exercise consistently reveals the accepted belief that feelers are sensitive and they are the only ones whose feelings get hurt. Thinkers tend to buy into the same belief. Since thinkers usually look down on feeling expressions, they make themselves believe that they do not succumb to such foolishness. However, once the group understands that I intend for them to complete the exercise, they go to work.

The group of thinkers scoring 45 or higher have difficulty identifying anything. After analyzing carefully, one high-scoring group of thinkers reported back to the group that feelers just weren't capable of hurting their feelings. They reported rationalizing the source if a feeler projected that they had erred. It took some time for them to see that they were rationalizing to avoid feeling.

Consistent messages from many groups showed the following responses from thinker preference groups about the way feelers hurt them. We selected representative statements from among the many participants. Thinkers say:

"Feelers expect us to have no pain."

"They manipulate us with their 'feel-good,' 'feel-bad' projections."

"Feelers make us feel guilty that we are not like them."

"They don't appreciate what we do. Just because we tend to show our feelings more by doing something for them rather than expressing verbally or affectionately, they discount our feelings."

"Feelers bring their problems to work and then fault me because I don't respond according to their expectations."

"They hold grudges and zap you from out of the blue."

"They use feelings as a cop-out. In a discussion when you have nailed them with objective facts, they retreat to emotion and treat us as persecutors for expecting them to be rational."

"They are so sensitive and moody you don't know how to approach them. They expect us to be able to read their feelings. They seem to think that their feelings set the norms for the interaction. We have to tiptoe through their emotional land mines. It's just not fair."

A sample of the ways feelers responded to the query about thinkers hurting their feelings shows the other side of the picture. Feelers say:

"Thinkers look down on us for having feelings."

"We want to be recognized as acceptable people."

"Thinkers are unresponsive and uncompassionate."

"They don't appear to care about us . . . they are aloof."

"Thinkers look for a way to get away when feelers have emotions."

"Thinkers treat us like children . . . instead of like equals . . . they are condescending."

"They don't show appreciation. Their idea of a real compliment is for you to go a month without their criticizing something you've done."

"Thinkers don't realize what pain they cause when they criticize or negate us. They don't seem to know that emotional pain hurts us physically and mentally as well."

"Thinkers think about tasks or ideas and don't seem to value tact."

"They hurt our feelings by not valuing our point-of-view . . . They interrupt, question us, and discount us."

After this exercise we take time to process the underlying messages and the desire of both thinkers and feelers to be understood and accepted. We then can talk about strategies to improve thinker-feeler interaction. The other piece of this exercise is to help each participant understand that the same desire to be understood and accepted goes on inside an individual. Remember: every one of us is both a thinker and a feeler. One of the processes is stronger than the other. An individual frequently feels the conflict between the rational and expressive messages. Being open to this internal dissonance in order to get the full picture of what's happening is part of confronting fear and becoming vulnerable in order to grow. Developing balance is not without cost.

THINKER-FEELER RESPONSE TO CONFLICT

Another workshop exercise that yields useful insight is identifying the typical process that thinkers and feelers use to respond to conflict. Working in small groups, they were asked to identify the way they typically handle a verbal criticism from someone.

Feelers identified a typical pattern that they used when someone criticized them:

Step 1: "Initial response is feel upset . . . feel crushed . . . Assume they don't like us."
Step 2: "We assume we're wrong . . . feel immediately guilty and childlike."
Step 3: "See their side."
Step 4: "Feel sorry for ourselves and begin asking 'Why did they crush us?' "
Step 5: "Defend ourselves with excuses."
Step 6: "Get the facts."
Step 7: "Get their reasons."
Step 8: "Apologize and try to smooth things over."
Step 9: "When it is too late, begin to analyze the situation and get a clearer perspective of the issue."

The thinker groups revealed very similar processes, whether

they were strong, moderate, or slight in their thinker preference scores. Common process used by thinkers when receiving a verbal criticism was reported as the following:

Step 1: "Ask for a clear statement of the problem."
Step 2: "Ask questions of what was done and why they perceive a problem."
Step 3: "Debate the problem statement."
Step 4: "Show where the logic is in error."
Step 5: "Debate the issue."
Step 6: "Work out a rational solution."
Step 7: "If a rational solution is refused, we consider the source and blow it off . . . unless it is the boss. If it's the boss, we monitor our persuasion accordingly. We don't particularly change our minds, but we reframe the question by including the cost factor. What will it cost us to be right? We can maintain the personal integrity of our own rationale and still bow to the boss's authority. It becomes the boss's problem if he uses inferior reasoning and then resorts to the power of position."

The thinker responds to criticism with questioning and judges the evidence supporting the assertion of fault. The feeler responds by initially accepting the assertion of fault and then later questioning and judging the evidence. The timing is reversed. The thinker pushes the criticism under the analytical microscope initially and later feels the feelings evoked by the criticism. The feeler feels the feelings initially and later analyzes the criticism.

A clear understanding of this difference is critical to leadership. Releasing human potential and building strength in people is the supreme task of a leader. A proper assessment of when and how to push the follower to maximum growth without destroying hope is the challenge.

In asking thinkers to discuss conflict in organizations, we found that thinkers have a real need to be treated fairly. The strong preference for logic leads to a strong value for justice. Here are some typical comments from thinkers about conflict:

"When pushed, I come out fighting hard with logic and reason as I see it."

"I like verbal volley on ideas, but I dislike personal attack. That is unethical."

"I hate people who argue dirty — bringing up emotional issues that are off the subject. My wife is an artist at that. We never can get a problem settled because she won't stay on the subject. Problems just become emotional battlegrounds. I can out-think her but she usually out-maneuvers me."

"I have a horrible temper if treated unfairly."

"I'm more confrontive than a feeler. I usually confront and then cut off a belabored emotional harangue."

Reviewing those rather typical thinker attitudes shows undeveloped feeler perspectives. The thinker judges feelings to be wrong and inferior and not legitimate fodder for the analytical machine.

Typical comments of feelers' attitudes toward conflict are:

"I avoid conflict at all costs."

"I just can't stand conflict. I get so upset I think I will explode. I experience a ringing in my ears, difficulty in breathing, and my throat starts to hurt."

"I feel like I wear a sign right out front that says 'If you don't stroke it, you hurt it.' "

"I think conflict is so hurtful to others. It's not right to inflict such pain."

"I love cooperation and agreement. Bickering and fighting is just a waste of time and energy."

One of the strongest values of feelers is harmony. You can see the pattern running through their comments. They value harmony, acceptance, absence of conflict, cooperation, and agreement. There is nothing weak about those values, unless you are willing to do anything to feel them.

The thinker wants to be treated fairly and impartially. The feeler wants to be treated personally and agreeably.

LEADERS BALANCE THINKING AND FEELING

Leaders frequently take actions that are not immediately perceived as fair, nor are they immediately perceived as agreeable. Leaders are charged with seeing further and more clearly than those they are leading. Leaders must be willing to endure the anger and frustration of those they lead, holding to the course until the led can see the wisdom of the action. Unfortunately, wisdom usually comes after the crisis has passed. Leaders must be strong enough to maintain clarity of purpose and vision even when no one else yet sees.

So thinkers must learn to accept feelings while thinking clearly, and feelers must learn to think clearly while feeling feelings. It sounds simple, but it is one of the most difficult human processes to master. Considering the pain, vulnerability, and risk involved in mastering thinking and feeling perspectives, it is understandable why typical American management has focused on one and avoided the other.

THINKER DEVELOPMENT OF FEELING AWARENESS

Thinkers value objectivity and have falsely reasoned that feeling data and objectivity are lethal enemies. Thinkers, then, face the challenge of learning to feel and process feelings without losing integrity of perception. We maintain that there is no integrity of perception without processing both rational and irrational content of situations. It may be irrational for workers to fear losing their jobs, but the irrational fear is a part of a rational assessment of the situation.

One thinker acknowledged that feelings were enemies to his being able to think clearly. He slowly began to acknowledge his fear that he would be so overwhelmed that he would do something stupid. When pressed for just what kind of stupid act he might commit, he found that he was afraid of showing emotion that would label him as weak, incapable, or unprofessional.

One of the maxims in the power game is, "If I can make you feel, I can take you out of the game." Spoken like a thinker! That maxim shows the fear of feelings. Barr and Barr asserts that fear of feelings makes you uniquely subject to manipulation. Fear of feelings usually drives you into the extreme position of sealing yourself off so strongly from feelings that you falsely conclude you don't have them or you find yourself avoiding them as much as you can. Either position weakens your ability to realistically assess a situation.

Thinkers then can be weakened by avoiding, denying, rationalizing, suppressing, or undervaluing feelings. They may appear rigid, pedantic, cold, impersonal, formal, and plastic in their responses.

The goal: thinkers must integrate feelings into their rationale. Clearly, we do not suggest that feelings dominate or control rationale. We say to integrate, not subordinate.

The goal: feelers must integrate clear cause-and-effect thinking into their rationale. We did not suggest that feelers should ignore their feelings and become thinkers. We suggest that feelers learn to maximize their natural ability as feelers to see the people situation and develop their thinker skills to see the principles involved in the situation.

Thinkers and feelers are challenged to master the following:

1. Attend to personal associations and feelings as part of the understanding of a situation or person; attend to principles, variables, and facts in the cause-effect relationships of the situation.
2. Appreciate as well as evaluate.
3. Avoid habitual skepticism or blind optimism by clearly assessing both positive and negative aspects of situations.
4. Integrate objectivity and compassion.
5. Express affection as well as criticism.
6. Evaluate when exceptions to a rule are equally as valid as the rule.
7. Personalize as well as analyze.

Exercises for Balance

1. Using a movie or television program, select a character and identify with that character. Try to feel the feelings of that character. Since it is a vicarious experience, you should be able to increase your awareness of feelings in your system. Halfway through, try to separate yourself from the character and analyze what the character is experiencing. This sort of practice should heighten your awareness about the other type of judgment.
2. Use inexpensive ways to explore feelings while trying to see cause-effect relationships. By inexpensive, we mean use low-risk situations such as movies, television, or music to practice opening up to feelings and clearly analyzing messages and moods.
3. Recall a situation at work. Relax and recall what the situation

felt like at the time. Don't rush into analyzing. Allow yourself
to feel the situation as it happened. When you have the feeling
content clear, list the principal feelings of each of the participants in the situation. Now, identify the variables that you
think were most significant in the situation. See if your reas-
sessment of the situation shows an integration of both the feelings and principles involved.
  4. Thinkers can find a low-risk person to practice verbalizing
     and expressing feelings. Feelers can find a low-risk person to
     practice expressing cause-effect analysis of a situation.
  5. Feelers can watch a trusted thinker's use of systematic inquiry
     in examining a problem.
  6. Thinkers can watch a trusted feeler's empathic handling of a
     potentially explosive situation.

CASE STUDY:
THINKER-FEELER DEVELOPMENT

When my feeler assistant takes a message on the phone, she re-
lays the message with an opening statement of the way the person
sounded on the phone and then gives me the message. In a call
from an anxious client, she said, "Mr. Thomas called. He was very
abrupt on the phone — not friendly at all. He didn't like me. He is
having trouble with the marketing man again and wants you to facilitate another meeting." She gave me the details of the message
after she had given me the disturbing effect Mr. Thomas had on
her. Feelers tend to be struck first with the agreeable-disagreeable-
ness of an interaction, and second with the task information.

By contrast, a message from one of my thinker employees was,
"Jones called about the pesticide coalition. He seemed to have
three issues: (1) the management report, (2) the legislative committee reactions, and (3) the timing of the litigation. He wants you to
give him a call at 459-3002." The thinker listened to the conversation and organized it according to cause and effect. He identified
the cause of the call, then identified the three issues mentioned in
the call. The information he gave me was then given in his logical
manner. When I asked him if the caller sounded upset, he looked at
me quizically and replied, "I have no idea."

Please do not deduce from the two examples that the feeler employee does not pick up content from the message, nor that the

thinker employee does not pick up feeling intent from the message. The examples were used to indicate priorities that the two use in processing information. When asked cause-and-effect questions, the feeler reexamines the content and gives the information. Similarly, the thinker can give some identifying information about the caller's emotional content.

When the thinker did not respond informatively to my query about the caller's emotional intent, I asked the question more specifically. "When you answered the call, did Jones chat a bit or did he open the conversation with a statement about the problem?" As I asked for specifics, the thinker could recall the conversation and respond to my questions. The thinker was not comfortable speculating about the emotional tone of the message, until I asked for specifics that allowed me to make the speculation. By asking the questions to which the thinker responded, the pressure for the thinker to speculate was switched to me. He was giving me the information, and I was inferring about the emotional tone.

An important task of management is development of employee potential. Finding ways to maximize their learning is challenging. One method available to the manager who can read basic patterns in employees is to find situations to expand their use of their less dominant side.

Sending two employees with different talents to do a task can be a method of developing employee potential. If there is an important meeting which I cannot attend, I sometimes send both a thinker and a feeler to the meeting. Though this appears to be an inefficient use of resources, I use this method to train each of them. I ask them to attend the meeting and give me their individual perspectives.

I ask them to make a joint verbal report on the meeting. During this session, I demonstrate the value of cause-effect information (the thinker specialty) and the value of observed people response at the meeting (the feeler specialty). Both types of information are essential in developing strategy. The debriefing of the reports allows the two employees to see the strengths of both thinker and feeler viewpoints. I then usually take time to show them how to weave both types of information into our company strategy. It is a handy on-the-job training opportunity. I close the session by reminding them the value of both perspectives and urge them to appreciate both ways of judging information. They become aware of the limits of a strategy that does not contain both the thinker-feeler information. After awareness, the next step is to continue their training until they develop skills for the perspective that is not quite as natural. Development of both thinker and feeler awareness is training for an essential characteristic for leadership: clear judgment.

The strong thinker preference is a natural for interpreting information from the impersonal cause-effect organization of information. The thinker appreciates logical approaches, objective descriptions, and consistent rational patterns. One thinker said, "I don't think it is fair to burden the decision-making process with people's feelings. I don't ask how people *feel* about a decision. I ask them what they *think,* and that is precisely what I want to know." Notice the thinker's judgment of feeling as a burden on the process. He is also demanding precision of analytical response, and in his judgment, precision excludes feeling content.

The strong feeler preference is a natural for interpreting information from the personal organization of information. The feeler appreciates information about people, their responses and values. The feeler appreciates sensitivity, tactfulness, and personal warmth. A feeler said, "I just can't work with a super critical person who is always putting others down. No matter how important they are to the project. I just don't think it's right to make others feel bad." Notice the feeler's judgment of wrong based upon hurting someone. The person was more important to the feeler than the project. The feeler may have been as dedicated to the project as anyone else; but when forced to choose between the project and upsetting people, not hurting people is more important than the project.

When great change occurs, most people feel pressure on the thinker-feeler dimension. The feeler may respond initially with intense emotional reaction to the change, and then at some point switch to cause-effect analysis that allows acceptance of the change. The thinker may respond initially with intense analytical detachment to the change and then at some point later get in touch with the emotional impact of the change. The thinker may be quite surprised to realize that s/he is emotionally opposed to the change, though the cause-effect analysis may have led to acceptance of the change.

Again, our preferences indicate the priority of the information in our consciousness, not the exclusivity of the information.

THINKER REACTION TO CRISIS

One of the most useful ways to determine whether you are a dominant thinker or feeler is to review your reactions to crisis. Think about a car wreck or some similar event. If you have not experienced an accident, then recall a physical emergency in order to check the validity of your preference.

In extreme situations, our natural preference tends to override its opposite, taking charge of the conscious processing of information. After the situation passes, the opposite information is processed.

Shortly after I began to learn about the applicability of the Myers-Briggs information, I recalled a car accident in which I had been involved. I suddenly understood the pattern of my reactions by looking at the thinker-feeler dimension.

CASE STUDY: THINKER VS. FEELER REACTIONS

Three of us were on our way to a meeting seventy miles from home. We decided to drive through the country to our destination. I was sitting in the back seat. The front left tire blew out, and the driver panicked and slammed on the brakes. We went into a roll, with the car overturning three times before coming to rest upside down. The driver was screaming hysterically. I was unaware of feelings.

I immediately saw in my mind's eye a picture of a car exploding in fire. I heard myself say in a cold, commanding voice, "Get your hand on the key and get the car turned off." The driver did not appear to hear me as she continued hysterically screaming. My voice became more direct and demanding, "Get your hand free and get it on the key and do it *now!*" The driver responded. First step of solving the problem was accomplished.

As I heard the engine turn off, my mind moved logically to the next step. Get us out of the car. As I recall the incident, I remember my voice softening and becoming more soothing as I assured the two people in the front seat that I would have us out of there in a few minutes. The seat upon which I had been sitting was now on top of me. I wiggled out from under the seat, again assuring the two crying passengers that I would get us out of the car and that everything would be all right. Now, I ask you: Who put me in charge of the wreck? We did not have a committee meeting to decide who would be in charge. My thinker preference automatically took over. We had a problem and I moved instinctively into my most trusted mode — thinker. My two friends moved into theirs — feeler. We aren't talking about a right or wrong way to respond to an accident. We are talking about the natural dominance of our preferences taking charge of our behavior in emergencies.

My side of the car was a few inches from a concrete culvert and the door would not open. I crawled across the car, got the other door open, then assured my friends that the door was open and I would have them out in a moment. At that moment my rationality allowed me to do an irrational thing. I scrambled around the back seat, found my sunglasses, put them on, and crawled out of the car. Sunglasses are not needed to get people out of a wrecked car. I had no idea at the time that I had done that. The replay much later dredged up from my memory that irrational act among the exceptionally rational sequence of events.

As soon as I got out of the car, I got the other two passengers out. I quickly assessed their injuries and knew stopping the bleeding was step one. After the bleeding was stemmed, I made them as comfortable as possible and told them I would go to a nearby farmhouse and take care of things.

As I hurried to the farmhouse, I systematically reviewed the phone calls necessary to take care of things. I called the highway patrol, giving them clear directions to our location, checked to make sure they were sending an ambulance, called the families of the other two, telephoned the chairman of the meeting I was supposed to attend, arranged with him to schedule the fourth speaker in my time slot, allowing me to speak later in the program, then called my family to assure them that all was well.

When the highway patrol and ambulance arrived and the situation was under control, my problem-solving nature moved on to the problem of following through on my commitment to speak at the meeting. Just about that time, a man stopped to see about the accident. He was an associate and recognized the car. I assured him that we were all right. I rode on to the meeting with him, gave my talk, chaired a committee meeting, and then went home. I telephoned the hospital and checked on my friends. So far, so good. I was not in touch with the emotional impact of the day's events. I felt fine that evening. The next day, while sitting at my desk, I reached for a cup of coffee. My hand began to shake and I spilled coffee on the report I was reading. The delayed feeling messages were demanding a hearing. As a thinker, I would rather talk about feelings than feel them.

During emergencies, thinkers tend to suppress the feeling content and focus instead on analytically solving the problem. My two friends are both feelers. The moment they realized that we were having an accident, they were immediately in touch with their feelings about the event. I was not in touch and did not experience feelings consciously until twenty-four hours later. After the emotional reaction passed, then my two friends went into problem-solving mode to respond to the abrupt change that the accident produced.

Later we were discussing our experiences about the accident. One friend remarked, "Norma, you were so calm during the whole thing. How did you do that?" At that time, I sensed the two of them subtly withdraw from me, but I didn't understand what was happening. Much later, with the help of the Myers-Briggs information, we talked again and I understood what they were thinking.

My two feeler friends were wondering if I weren't a little too detached from their feelings. They were interpreting my actions during the accident as evidence that I may not care as much about them as they thought. They saw and felt my actions as being "too cool and too collected." As feelers, their natural style is to judge people by their reactions to them. We talked at length about my style of solving the problem as a way of caring about them. They admitted that they wished that I had been more gentle and that I had sat with them a bit longer before I raced off for the farmhouse to make the phone calls. They would have felt more assurance of my genuine concern for them. That discussion gave me valuable insight into the different reactions of feelers and thinkers.

Many times executives have discussed with us the problem of others seeing them as too controlled and too objective. In the business setting, they found those statements complimentary. At home, however, the same statements were hurtful and they believed were inaccurate.

CASE STUDY: CONTROLLED THINKER

A senior corporate vice-president whom we will call Tom shared the following example:

When our son cut the artery in his leg, I knew that time was essential. I didn't have time to worry about anyone's feelings. We had a serious situation and I took charge. While my wife and I were waiting for our son to come out of surgery, I tried to console her but found her distant and unresponsive. The next day, I canceled two important appointments in order to go to the hospital to see my son. As I approached the door, I overheard my wife and son talking. He said, "Dad seemed really mad at me for hurting myself." My wife responded, "Oh, I'm sure Dad cares about you. It's just his way. He nearly bit my head off when I asked him where the keys were when he was putting you in the car. I wish he showed his love more, but I know he loves us."

As Tom told the experience, he relived the emotion that he felt at the time.

I was so upset at what they were saying, I felt my knees start to wobble and my vision got fuzzy. I made my way down the hall and went into the waiting room until I could get control again. I felt anger at the way they misunderstood my actions. I felt hurt that they could be so blind to my real feelings. I felt justified in ordering them about during the emergency. I felt sick at the picture they were painting of me. Then I hastily remembered I had just canceled two important appointments. Surely, that was proof of their importance to me.

We discussed the thinker preference of problem-solving that frequently appears to others as detached coolness. Thinkers can become so habituated to problem-solving that the less-skilled feeler doesn't get as much expression. Thinkers feel deeply, but are much less likely to communicate those feelings.

The busy executive felt deeply about his wife and son. He told me emphatically about the decisions he had made because of his love for them. He discussed his anger that they could not figure out his true feelings. As he calmed down, he began to see his own pattern. He had been expecting them to rationally deduce from the series of actions that he was indeed very loving. Both his son and his wife wanted to *see* and *feel* that he cared. They wanted an "irrational" demonstration of caring that they could feel. Tom looked stricken as he said, "I'm no good at that mushy stuff. It comes out so phony."

We discussed the importance of developing skills for our opposite side. At first, communicating feelings may feel as awkward as putting on a pair of snow skis for the first time, or trying to write with your least favorite hand. It feels awkward, phony, uncomfortable. That risky phase is an essential part of developing skills in an area that is not your first preference. Thinkers need to find ways to communicate genuine feelings instead of hiding behind their preference for detachment and objectivity. Attachment and subjectivity also have their place in communication.

Most of us can see the need for attachment and subjectivity at home, but we have been trained as managers to see feeler expressions as threats to our professionalism.

CLEAR ASSESSMENT OF BOTH THINKER AND FEELER INFORMATION

Working with Tom gave us the opportunity to see more of how his thinker preference worked. His staff described working with him: "He's tough"; "He'll nail you if you don't have your facts right"; "He can cut you to shreds in a few seconds." (Remember: Leadership is measured by the effect on the led.)

As an ISTJ (introvert, sensor, thinker, judge) executive, Tom was interested in facts, logic, and control. As an introvert, he did not like to "waste time" thinking aloud. Tom scored in the upper 40s and 50s on all four dimensions — a man of strong preferences.

Tom thought deeply about things, but rarely shared his thought processes with others. Neither did he give much feedback. Staff gave him information and he appeared to assimilate it, but rarely did he remember to tell others what he had done with their information. He assumed that people could see the impact of their information upon the decisions he made. This was a poor assumption. Tom continually missed opportunities to inspire and motivate others because of his strong personal preferences for terse, targeted communication. Tom's staff and his family perceived the toughness. Tom's feelings were so intensely private that they rarely showed on the surface.

THINKER VS. FEELER INFORMATION

Objective, rational thinking is valued in organizational settings. Such skill is frequently overvalued; whereas, people sensitivity is sometimes undervalued in organizations. Feeler communication is frequently seen as less powerful and, therefore, less important. Rationality and emotionality are not adjudged the same in business and organizational settings. Even in social service organizations whose mission clearly states helping others, I have seen objective rationality appear far stronger than value-oriented presentations. Please note that the word "appear" for evaluating long-term effects in terms of both people and work is necessary before we conclude thinking more valuable than feeling. A decision is not an effective decision until it is implemented. The rational decision still has to be accepted and implemented by people.

Both feeler and thinker aspects of a decision are important; however, feeler comments are frequently discounted in meetings.

CASE STUDY: THINKER-FEELER

Barr and Barr submitted an organizational audit to a company's board of directors. We were present at the meeting to answer questions and facilitate the discussion. In calling for response to the report, the chairman of the board asked for opening positions of support or dissent. He was clearly asking for position statements followed by reasons and discussion issues.

The one feeler on the fifteen-person board raised his hand and said, "I fully support the entire report. It is a wonderful report. Difficult issues were treated sensitively and factually. I really liked it and feel good about it."

As he talked, the subtle reaction of other board members was interesting. They gave nonverbal indications of withdrawing attention to the comments. The feeling, value-laden words (wonderful, sensitively, feel good) appeared to the analyticals as invalidation of the board member's point of view. The nonverbal cues from which we inferred their judgment were (1) people turning away from the speaker, (2) members opening the report in front of them, (3) many withdrawing eye contact, (4) some exchanging judgmental glances, (5) three separate whispered conversations beginning, (6) the chairman looking at his watch, and (7) the secretary appearing to be waiting with pen poised for content to enter into the minutes.

Feelers have too often experienced the discounting of their positions. When their personal priorities and feelings about issues get taken apart by logical analysis, the dissection usually feels personal. It feels like a personal attack, more than an objective discussion of ideas.

When people with strong feeler preference discuss issues, they tend to use subjective and human values. They usually feel proud of being able to feel an issue as well as talk about it. Feelers usually come to conclusion about issues by an associative process. As the various elements of the issue are discussed, feelers associate past experiences of similar emotional impact, stories they have heard, and emotional cues of the elements of the problem. As the discussion proceeds, feelers tend to arrange the elements according to compassion and responsiveness to people's needs. Thinkers in the same discussion tend to arrange the elements according to cause-and-effect possibilities. There are times when an observer might wonder if the thinker and feeler were involved in the same discussion.

CASE STUDY:
THINKER-FEELER STRATEGY

We observed a five-person management team dealing with a complicated situation. As a chemical services company, they offered services to a number of clients. The client involved in the current crisis was a criminal justice department of probation. The company did screening tests for the probation department to determine chemical content in urinalysis. The employee involved in the situation being discussed had been hired by the company specifically as a part of the team that serviced the probation contract. The problem: the female employee, who was four months pregnant, was told by her physician that she must not handle urine specimens during the term of the pregnancy. She had asked the company for a reassignment. Her supervisor had just been notified of a budget cut and told employees they would not be laid off but resigning employees would not be replaced, thereby using attrition as the staff adjustment mechanism.

When the supervisor checked with her boss to determine if reassignments fell under the attrition rule, she was told that they did. If the employee did not perform urinalysis, then she would no longer be complying with her job assignment. If she did not wish to comply, then she should seek other employment. The supervisor tried to get an exception for the rule but was unable to do so. The supervisor was upset with the decision. Wanting to get the unpleasant situation over with quickly, she went back to the employee and told her that if she could not perform the job, then she would have to quit.

The pregnant employee, a feeler, left the supervisor's office crying. When she got to her desk, several people gathered around to see what the problem was. She then told them that she was being fired because she was pregnant. That rumor flew through all fourteen locations of the company in about five minutes.

The chemical company was operated by an STJ (sensor, thinker, judge) organizational style. The typical style was to check the facts, analyze them objectively, and decide quickly. The supervisor and her boss responded accordingly. They underestimated the potentially explosive emotional issue of pregnancy and fairness. Motherhood was not the emotional variable to discount.

Typically, people accuse organizations of insensitivity and are eager to find evidence of the heartlessness of managerial decisions. They tend to look for evidence that shows profit as the motive and insensitivity as the norm.

Two hours after the supervisor talked to the employee about finding another job, the five-person executive team was hastily strategizing about squelching the fire of rumor and anger that was igniting across the company. In just two hours, the labor union representative demanded a meeting; the chief of probation with whom they had the contract called demanding an explanation; the district judge who chairs the probation board called to see if they were clear of litigious possibility; the employee's personal lawyer called and asked for a meeting; the woman's husband called and threatened to take out a full-page newspaper ad denouncing the company; and five department heads phoned, asking for information to settle the emotionality of the situation.

In the organizationally intense environment of budget constraints and staff cut-back, the forest was already dry and ready for an emotional spark to set off the fears, concerns, and angers.

The problem was immediately taken to the executive team. They began their discussion by trying to get the facts straight. They had to recheck a number of facts to reconstruct the happenings and the sequence of events as they actually happened. As they reviewed the decision rationale, four of them concurred that the decision was logical. They reasoned:

CAUSE:	The employee has a problem meeting job description.
PREMISES:	The company is not responsible for employee's condition.
	The doctor's advice was between doctor and employee.
	The job description takes precedence over individual situation of the employee.
	Cutbacks are necessary.
	The employee's pregnancy made her unable to fulfill her job duties.
CONCLUSION:	Her resignation would be seen as her choice.
	Her position falls under the rules of attrition.
	Her job will not be refilled.

The four people concluded that they supported the decision rationale. The fifth person on the team, a woman who scored 31 as a feeler, stated a different point of view. Ann is a natural feeler but a trained thinker. She carefully followed the logical approach of her colleagues, then introduced a realistic assessment. "No matter how comfortable you might be with the decision rationale, you have a different issue to address now. The dominant issue here is company attitude toward people. They are saying we are cold, unfair, and insensitive."

A colleague interrupted, "Hey, we didn't get to these positions because we needed the world to love us."

Ann replied, "You miss my point. The way we respond to this problem is going to be carefully scrutinized. If we hide behind our decision rationale without genuinely responding to the misunderstanding, we could pay for it in lowered morale, lawsuits, equipment sabotage, cancellation of our contract, and badly damaged trust."

"Oh, come on, Ann. It's not that serious."

Ann responded, "Just how serious do you think motherhood, justice, and the American way is, Al?"

The president of the company intervened, "Ann, I think I see your point. You are saying we are taking an analytically cold look at this issue and are underestimating the potency of feelings already aroused."

"Right. We must respond to the emotional message first before we can hope to solve the problem."

The executive team then devised a quick strategy. They decided to use the explosive situation as an opportunity to demonstrate their willingness to learn. They divided the locations between them and all five of them left right after the meeting to go to various locations of the company. Fortunately, all locations could be visited that day. Their strategy included the following steps:

1. Show the responsiveness of the executive team by going to the sites to immediately demonstrate their concern.
2. Don't defend the company but rather focus on letting the people express their thoughts and feelings (it could be a rich opportunity to drain off some stress resulting from not being heard).
3. Notify department heads of their arrival and ask for an informal meeting with employees.
4. Promise to respond to the situation within forty-eight hours.
5. Promise to come back to explain their decision.
6. President would personally call the union representative and the probation chief and explain their rationale with the pledge to respond within forty-eight hours. He would also call the judge, the employee, and the lawyer.

The president's call and his pledge to get back to them as soon as possible — and certainly within forty-eight hours — with more information brought a conciliatory response from most. The union representative and the employee voiced doubt about the outcome but begrudgingly agreed to wait forty-eight hours before taking further action.

Ann quickly reminded them that genuine listening and respect for other people's view of the situation were critical parts of their response. She valued each of the members of the executive team and felt confidence that they could and would control their usually judgmental, analytical, critical approaches and would instead discipline themselves to truly trying to feel and sense the situation. She also trusted their analytical skill to ask leading questions to help clarify the situation and buy time by demonstrating their desire to sort out the misunderstanding.

The executive team agreed to meet at 8:30 that evening to compare their findings and develop their response.

That evening the executive team shared its assessment of the situation. They agreed that a caring response to the employee's request was now more important than the rule of attrition and the budget concern. By checking the situation carefully, they found a comparable lab job in another department, where they were testing the effects of an anesthesia formula for dental patients. They negotiated an agreement with one of the lab employees working on the dental tests to trade places with the pregnant employee until after the birth of the child. Fortunately, the jobs were equal in pay and benefits.

When the executive team reached the solution to the problem, they carefully attended to each of the potentially explosive factions caught up in the issue. The president personally called each of the principal parties. Then the team negotiated the change between the two employees, between the two supervisors involved, and between the two department heads. As soon as agreement and implementation details had been worked out, they set up meetings with all employees again.

One member of the executive team argued that their taking time to go back to each location seemed wasteful to him. He was outvoted by the others. They reminded him that follow-through on their commitment was essential. They also realized that their going back would give them a grass-roots feel for whether or not their solution was acceptable. They saw the visits with employees as essential in assessing the acceptability of their decision and in demonstrating managerial commitment.

The combination of analytical skills of the thinkers and people savvy of the feeler enabled the executive team to respond in a more effective way to the crisis.

Let's review the strengths and weaknesses of both the strong feeler and thinker preferences. We'll review feeler preference first.

FEELER STRENGTHS AND WEAKNESSES

STRENGTH:	Likes to support and give to others
WEAKNESS:	May give and support indiscriminately

Example: The feeler manager's personal interest in employees may result in a strong commitment to help employees. S/he may get so caught up in the personal aspect of the situation that employees might take advantage of the manager. Too much giving and support invites manipulation.

STRENGTH:	Shares emotional sensitivity
WEAKNESS:	May collect too much emotional data and become overloaded with feelings that distort perception

Example: A feeler manager became quite involved in helping one of his employees during the employee's divorce. The feeler manager rescued the weary parent when first the car broke down, then one of the children became ill, then the employee became deeply depressed. The manager tried to cheer up the employee and allow as much time off as possible. He assumed too much of the employee's burden and soon found himself tired, irritable, and depressed also. It seemed the more he helped the employee with personal problems, the more problems he found. The feeler manager was trying to ease the pain and wasn't addressing the causes of the pain.

STRENGTH:	Behaves demonstratively and expressively
WEAKNESS:	May give away too much information, time, and energy

Example: The previous example demonstrates this point. As the manager sought more ways to help the employee, more and more time was spent. The manager even shared some of his own experience about a divorce. He gave the employee too much personal information, which was later used against him. It was also used by the employee to make him feel guilty with hints that he should be more helpful since he knew what it felt like to be so upset.

STRENGTH:	Sees the people perspective; interprets events as they affect people
WEAKNESS:	May oversimplify; may overpersonalize

Example: A feeler supervisor was told about two incidents of security breach by one of her employees. The employee's father was dying of cancer, and the supervisor felt compassion for the pain and struggle. The employee had failed to secure the private files before leaving work. When the supervisor talked to the employee about the problem, the employee tearfully excused the oversight as a part of her stress.

The third time the problem occurred, the supervisor's boss called her about the situation. She simplified the problem by rearranging it as "a little matter of leaving files on top of her desk." Her boss was quick to remind her that the policy of securing private files was longstanding and quite serious. The feeler supervisor agreed to do something about it. When she hung up the phone, she said, "He didn't have to chew me out; he could have just talked to me about it." She had rationalized the errors and excused her own response to the problem. Because the employee was experiencing a painful situation, the supervisor failed to see the abdication of responsibility. She saw the pain as a reasonable excuse for the abdication.

STRENGTH:	Charms and persuades
WEAKNESS:	May rely too much on charm and not enough on preparation

Example: One intuitive feeler manager was just so charming that he disarmed most opposition with his good humor and ready wit. He continually tried to "wing it" rather than do disciplined preparation for important presentations. As a result, he became unpredictable to his boss. At times, the manager would represent the company brilliantly, and at other times he would appear unprepared and disorganized.

STRENGTH:	Can hook people's initial interest (sales, presentations, conversations)
WEAKNESS:	May take too long getting to the main point; may make the main point too imprecise to be understood; may be too disorderly in presenting information

Example: John was effective at getting appointments. In the first few minutes he could make a warm personal approach that disarmed the other person and set a positive mood for the interaction. John could ramble around among untargeted statements until the other person became irritated at the waste of time.

STRENGTH:	Gives a descriptive account of a situation or event
WEAKNESS:	May tell too many anecdotes and stories

Example: Ann scored 35 as a feeler. Her boss scored 49 as a thinker. When they discussed their differences on the thinker-feeler dimension, the boss told Ann he valued her people savvy. He called her into his office and asked her to check on the computer integration between accounting and marketing. There were some delays which he suspected might be personal conflict rather than system installation problems. He asked her to check into it and brief him on what she found.

Ann reported back in forty-eight hours with her account of the situation. Ann confirmed that a power struggle was occurring. She went into detail about the struggle that had apparently begun eight years earlier. By the time Ann began to talk about today's incidents, her boss was so annoyed he could hardly listen. When he used the phrase "brief me on what you find," he had a different interaction in mind. He was expecting a clear statement of the findings and a logical list of influencing elements. By the time he listened to the scenario with detailed description of the stories, he reduced his respect for Ann's people savvy. She brought him too much "trivia" mixed in with the report of the situation.

STRENGTH:	Willingly overextends to help, as s/he identifies with people's feelings
WEAKNESS:	May "burn out" and drop into self-pity; may overreact and hold grudges

Example: Comments by people who work with Tom include: "Tom is a real person"; "He's a great guy"; "Always willing to help." People like Tom. His boss had relied on him many times when a deadline was imminent and extra hours were needed to meet it. They were facing another of those crises on Friday. Tom, as usual, volunteered to work as many nights as it took to meet the deadline. Additionally, he was letting a co-worker ride to work with him because the man's car was malfunctioning. Tom had been running a few errands for his rider after work on their way home. Also, Tom's son had volunteered him to referee the practice soccer game on Thursday evening. And Tom's aging mother had been calling to see if he would stop by to do a few chores for her. She reminded him, "You are such a good son. I don't know how I could get along without you."

Realizing that things were crowding in on him, Tom decided he would work as long as it took on Wednesday night on the project so he could be available for the Thursday night game. If he skipped dinner, he could stop at his mother's after work, do her chores, and make it to the game.

Tom worked until 1:15 A.M. before realizing that he couldn't finish that night. He went home tired. He was in the office thirty minutes early the next morning to start again. By 11:00 A.M. he realized the work was going too slowly. Someone was going to have to work tonight to get it finished by the Friday deadline.

The boss's secretary walked up to Tom and gave him a message, "I'm checking the schedule for this evening. Can we still count on you this evening?"

Tom said to the secretary, "I'm about the only one you can count on around here. I wish people would do their fair share. I'm sick of people leaving early while a few of us get the job done."

The secretary recognized the underlying message and replied, "Tom, maybe you'd better take this evening off. I'll see if we can find someone else to work this evening."

Tom said, "I told you I'd work and I will. I'm going to have to disappoint my family again, but that's nothing new."

Tom was so tired and angry that he was not willing to admit his overload. Instead he continued to make passive aggressive comments, get a reaction, then deny the intent. He was so into his martyrdom that he chose to enjoy his anger rather than admit it. Tom had so overscheduled himself in his willingness to help that he projected the blame for overscheduling onto others. Blaming others fueled his sense of self-righteousness. To accept the offer of someone else working that evening, Tom would have to give up his self-righteous anger. He chose to fuel it instead.

STRENGTH:	Likes to communicate
WEAKNESS:	May spend too much time in conversation

Example: A strong feeler draws energy from conversation and sharing. The enjoyment of interacting with people can supersede the goal of getting the work done.

Patty is a bright, talented young supervisor. She has high energy and a zest for living. Her manager asked us to take a look at Patty's job and her supervisory skills. Patty was complaining of work overload. She usually was at her desk until 6:30 or 7:00 in the evening "getting caught up."

It didn't take long to see what was happening. Patty spent much of her day wandering through the organization. She'd stop to help an employee and then stay to chat. She prided herself on her style of "managing by wandering around." What she overlooked was the time wasted in idle conversation. She quickly defended the conversation as building morale.

Patty had excuses for each of the observations about ineffective use of her time. Every observation I made, she excused. Finally, I recounted six conversations of a personal nature. She looked at me and said, "You're telling me that I'm doing too much socializing and not enough supervising."

I said, "That's what I am saying." I then discussed with her the expectations she was building for her employees, the model she was setting, and the inefficiency that was rampant in her unit. We discussed the change from social needs to managerial competency, developed a plan for her to discipline her social nature, and set clear, measurable goals for her supervisory approach.

Six months later, Patty had improved the unit's efficiency by 24%. She was very proud as she said, "You really hurt my feelings when you told me to quit wasting so much time talking. Even at that time, though, I knew it was true. I just didn't want to hear it. But look at us now. We're going to improve our efficiency another 10%. It's hard for me to watch my conversation, but it's worth it."

STRENGTH:	Likes cooperation
WEAKNESS:	May deny and smooth things over to avoid conflict

Example: John prided himself on the family feeling he demanded in his work group. When someone became quarrelsome, he quickly called that person aside and gave his pep talk about getting along together. His pep talk usually concluded with compliments for the disgruntled employee and the following statement: "I would take it as a personal favor to me, if you would make sure this is a pleasant and happy place to work."

One of the employees was a manipulative controller. Mary Alice figured out that John couldn't tolerate conflict. When she wanted something done her way, she only had to threaten to get upset and John would begin to concede. Occasionally, she actually raised her voice, but most of the time she could get what she wanted with subtle innuendo.

Other employees were annoyed with John for being unwilling to confront Mary Alice. They frequently had to do the more unpleasant tasks because Mary Alice refused. The manipulation involved Mary Alice subtly threatening John, he capitulated, and the other employees were expected to do whatever it took to keep her happy.

Feeler

STRENGTHS	WEAKNESSES
Likes to support and give to others	May give and support indiscriminately
Shares emotional sensitivity	May collect too much emotional data and become overloaded with feelings that distort perception
Behaves demonstratively and expressively	May give away too much information, time, and energy
Sees the people perspective; interprets events as they affect people	May oversimplify and overpersonalize
Charms and persuades	May rely too much on charm and not enough on preparation
Can hook people's initial interest	May take too long getting to the main point; may be too imprecise to get the message across; may be too disorderly in presenting information
Gives a descriptive account of a situation or event	May tell too many anecdotes and stories
Willingly overextends to help, as s/he identifies with people's feelings	May "burn out" and drop into self-pity; may overreact and hold grudges
Likes to communicate	May spend too much time in conversation

THINKER STRENGTHS AND WEAKNESSES

STRENGTH:	Prefers the analytical, logical expression
WEAKNESS:	May analyze instead of internalize while trying to avoid emotional expression

Example: The employee says, "I'm really upset about the sales department getting ten new word processors. They got new filing cabinets and four new desks two months ago. We work just as hard as they do, and we don't get anything."

Thinker boss responds, "It's a simple matter of the bottom line — sales are the reason we are in business. I give the guys who are bringing in the money top priority. It's a common rule of business."

The thinker boss rearranged the message, deleting the feeling message and responding with cold rationale.

STRENGTH:	Values logic
WEAKNESS:	May undervalue feelings in motivating people

Example: The thinker's overvaluing of logic rests on the belief that if people have a logical reason they will comply. This belief overlooks the reality of feelings as motivators.

The thinker boss in the previous example overlooked an opportunity to motivate the employee who was expressing feelings about a perceived unfair allocation of resources. The thinker boss did not realize that his cold rationale had conveyed to the employee the feeling message that the sales group was more important. In reciting the rationale, the boss put down the employee and his work group.

STRENGTH:	Handles emergencies logically
WEAKNESS:	May appear cold, insensitive, and uncaring

Example: A feeler phoned her thinker husband at work. She was crying and talking incoherently. The following dialogue occurred:

Thinker: "Stop that crying and speak clearly."
Feeler: "He's bleeding and I can't make it stop. I've . . ."
Thinker: "Calm down. Where are you?"

Feeler: "I'm in the kitchen and Tommy's crying and bleeding."
Thinker: "What happened? Tell me precisely where he is bleeding and describe the way the blood is coming out."
Feeler: "I don't know! It's all over his leg."
Thinker: "Get hold of yourself! Tell me exactly what it looks like. Tell me right now!"
Feeler: "It's gushing out in quick spurts."

The thinker seeks precise description to determine how to solve the problem. The thinker is overriding the feelings in order to establish order and clarity in the situation.

After the emergency is handled and the little boy's leg has been stitched up, the thinker begins to probe for the details about the accident. The direct questioning can be seen and felt by others as cold, insensitive, and uncaring.

STRENGTH:	Explains thoroughly and probes deeply into an issue
WEAKNESS:	May overexplain and ask too many questions

Example: At a management meeting, the CEO hastily called four department heads together. A customer called, very upset about the way his order was handled. The CEO did not want to lose the customer and wanted to immediately solve the problem and communicate the solution to the customer. His department heads were from sales, shipping, customer relations, and accounting.

Jim Sanders was the accounting department head. He had scored 45 in his preference for thinking on the Myers-Briggs.

As the problem unfolded, the communication breakdown occurred between sales and shipping. Jim, however, became intrigued with the problem. As the sales and shipping men were describing their department's handling of the problem, Jim took over the interaction and assumed the role of Grand Inquisitor. He began asking probing questions. He is referred to as the logician. Jim was so authoritative in his masterful questioning that the others were slow to realize he was asking questions not directly related to the current problem. Jim was caught up in his own single-minded probe of the situation and was quickly losing sight of the urgency of the situation.

After fifteen minutes of Jim's cross-examination of the two

men, the CEO interrupted: "Let's get back on track here. We identified the problem. I'm not interested in establishing beyond a reasonable doubt who screwed up. I'm interested in what we are going to do to fix it and how we are going to make sure this doesn't happen again."

Jim was annoyed. He thought he was helping to solve the problem. He did not see that he had become so involved in his own enjoyment of analyzing the problem that he had lost sight of the group objective.

As he went back to his office, an employee asked him to sign a report that needed to be in the morning mail. Jim took the report, which he had reviewed previously, and began a meticulous explanation of the form of the report. He went into detail about the format, changes he was considering making in it, comparisons with previous reports. He went on and on until the employee interrupted him with the information that the delivery person was waiting in his office to deliver the report.

Jim was unaware that indulgence in his thinker preference was blinding him to the real intent of interactions.

STRENGTH:	Prefers to keep remarks objective and impersonal
WEAKNESS:	May try to force feelings into what they *should* be or suppress them so they do not interfere with objective, rational expression; may appear insincere and unaffectionate

Example: Alan scored 51 on thinker preference and 35 on introvert preference on the Myers-Briggs. He was uncomfortable expressing feelings. His best forte was analyzing feelings.

One of his employees had just gone through a personal tragedy. The employee's infant daughter had died of "crib death." He got the message at work and rushed home. Alan walked by the employee's desk and noted that he was not working. He questioned another employee and discovered the emergency. He responded: "My that is quite a tragedy. I wonder if he told anyone where he put that report that's due in the morning. We better check on that. Tom, you see if you can find it. If you can't, I'll get in touch with him to see where it is. I know he wouldn't want to let that fall through the cracks. We will look after things here while he deals with this."

Alan's response to the situation was almost devoid of externalized feeling. His analytical mind quickly abstracted the impact on the work and moved to control that.

When the employee called Alan to tell him that he would not be back to work for a week, Alan responded with what he thought was a correct response. "We all know how you feel. You are caught up in the shock of all this. But time will heal everything. We will be glad when you get this taken care of and come back to work. You'll feel better when things get back to normal."

Alan was scrambling for expressions that were appropriate. He put together trite responses that covered his discomfort with the emotional intensity of the situation instead of risking genuine expression of sympathy.

Alan was afraid to express genuine sympathy, afraid of being overwhelmed by his own feelings. He had such undeveloped feeling function that he saw feelings as a terrible threat to his rationality. In his mind, feelings would blot out his ability to think. He had not developed the ability to feel tremendous feelings and think clearly simultaneously. He was stuck with the fear that it could not be done. Thus, Alan came off as being insincere.

Alan's wife and children see him as unaffectionate. When the youngest child skidded on a gravel pathway, skinned his leg badly, and came crying into the house, Alan questioned him severely. The child was crying and bleeding and Alan was firing the questions about why the accident occurred. "Where were you when this happened? Were you riding your bike on that gravel again? You know better than that. Why weren't you looking where you were going?" The questions would have continued until Alan got a satisfactory case built against the child if his wife had not interrupted.

"Alan, the child is bleeding. You can get your righteous satisfaction after I get him cleaned up," she said.

Alan's immediate response to the situation was to discern the wrongdoing of the child. His wife's response was to the child.

STRENGTH:	Likes a formal approach
WEAKNESS:	May be overly formal

Example: The thinker's preference for objectivity may induce a formal approach to others. The thinker may be overly formal in meeting new people.

Janice took great pride in her role as a lawyer. When meeting people, she was quite correct in her greeting. She concentrated on correct pronunciation of names and establishing clear roles. She was seen by others as being stiff and too formal.

Thinker

STRENGTHS	WEAKNESSES
Prefers the analytical, logical expression	May analyze instead of internalize while trying to avoid emotional expression
Values logic	May undervalue feelings in motivating people
Handles emergencies logically	May appear cold, insensitive
Explains thoroughly and probes deeply into an issue	May overexplain and ask too many questions
Prefers to keep remarks objective and impersonal	May try to force feelings into what they *should* be or *suppress* them so they do not interfere with objective, rational expression; may appear insincere and unaffectionate
Likes a formal approach	May be overly formal

Remember: everyone has both thinker and feeler communication channels. One of them is dominant. Maximizing the natural preference and developing skills for its opposite is the route to balanced type development and is critical to leadership.

Thinkers tend to believe that they respond to intellectually considered, rationally sound motives. This leads to the conclusion that their opinion is based upon clear principles and objective application of those principles. They believe that their opinions are based upon valid reasoning; therefore, anyone who disagrees must be incorrect, unreasonable, or not quite smart enough to think clearly. The exception to this belief in their own opinion comes when a thinker develops the feeler balance to provide a whole picture.

Feelers tend to believe that they respond to human factors of a situation with great clarity. They see the problem as a people issue and frame their solution from that perspective. This leads to the conclusion that their opinion is based upon right (as opposed to wrong) concerns for the people involved. They believe their opinions are based upon valid concern for the whole situation; therefore, anyone who disagrees must be wrong, cold, or not caring enough to see the problem as it should be seen. The exception to this opinionated belief comes when a feeler develops the thinker balance to provide a whole picture.

FEELER SENSITIVITY

One feeler described what it is like to be a feeler:

I never know when I am going to be filled up with emotion. At its worst, my chest fills up, my throat becomes tight. My emotions trap me. I want to tear off my body and get rid of them. I can't stop them.

There is a range of emotions from mild to intense. Sometimes I am emotional with no identifiable reason. I feel "edgy," my throat and chest feel uncomfortable and tears come easy. The feelings don't have thought forms with them. I can't identify why I am upset. The other extreme is when I am so overwhelmed with feelings that I can't think. My mind feels blank . . . detached . . . as if I can't get to it, to use it. Intense feelings interfere with concentration.

When I feel intensely emotional, the feelings build and build until I can cry a lot and then it releases. I have had crying periods without an identifiable cause at the time. Later, I begin to realize that I was responding to someone else's feelings and was feeling the anxiety and weight as if they were mine.

When I get the release after crying, I feel so relieved. My chest doesn't hurt anymore, my muscles release and I can get on with what I'm doing.

I feel two kinds of emotional waves. One kind just comes up so strong I can't stop it. The other kind is one that comes on more slowly and I have time to make a choice. I can choose to try to relax into it or I can indulge and let it come on strong. I know when I am going overboard and indulging in my feelings.

After I've had a strong emotional experience and I've

gotten the release, the intensity has already passed, I have to decide not to wallow in the feeling.

I've learned some things that help me. I found that most of the time, I make a decision whether to try to close feelings off, bury them, or open up and feel them. When I say open up and feel them, I don't mean wallow in them. I mean try to stay calm and realize that they will pass. If you are a feeler, you are going to have to wrestle with feelings continually. I think it helps to recognize feeling patterns:

(1) expect feelings . . . know they are going to come;
(2) release feelings . . . know they are going to go;
(3) just ride them out . . . like a roller coaster;
(4) don't take them out on other people . . . just ride them out without hurting anyone;
(5) learn about the downhill slide into a depressed cycle . . . the cycle is something like (a) worried about messing up, (b) think I did, (c) get angry at myself, (d) become tense and upset, (e) become afraid that I'm going to become really depressed, and (d) be sad and depressed.

I've learned to be more aware of this cycle so I can see it starting and do something about it.

This feeler is quite perceptive and is able to verbalize the process of feeling. Other feelers reviewed this description and found it apt. You can also see the thinker development in the feeler description. Though she scores as a strong feeler on the Myers-Briggs, she is actively developing her thinker balance. You can see evidence of her thinker approach in identifying the process of feeling.

THINKER ASPECT OF FEELING

A thinker talked about the struggle with feelings from a different perspective. He talked about the absence of feelings and his inability to know what he was feeling much of the time. He is a young professional whose college training further reinforced his propensity for an analytical approach to life. He is approaching his role of supervision with the same type of preference.

The thinker said the following:

I am really turned off when someone comes on with emotional, circular thinking. They talk all around a subject and never get to the point. I would like for them to state the problem and give me the facts. They want to stay on the flavor instead of the facts.

I have trouble understanding where they are coming from. I try to keep my feelings under control so they do not interfere. If I get too much feeling, I get confused.

My mind stays very busy, analyzing and figuring things out. I don't have time to sit around and feel.

You see that this thinker is uncomfortable with feelings and clearly sees them producing inferior information to his "clean rationality." After more discussion, he finally got in touch with his fear of feeling too much. He talked about his fear of the chaotic effect on his ability to think when his feelings were too strong; therefore, he tried to keep them suppressed. He was so cautious about letting too many of his feelings register in his consciousness that he could go long periods of time when he felt very little. He described it as being numb:

I know what I should feel, but at times I just can't do it. I try to act like I think I should, but frequently I don't feel it. When too many feelings occur, I feel as if I am going crazy. It's awful. My reality changes with the feelings and I know I am becoming irrational. I'm more cautious about negative feelings, but positive feelings affect my objectivity also. I really admire people who can stay calm and proceed logically.

Whether you are a dominant thinker or feeler, tremendous potential lies in the other side of the judging process. Clear thinking requires you to process both types of information.

— 6 —

Control:
Judge-Perceiver

The need to control is one of the major issues to consider in the judge-perceiver dimension. Managers scoring high on the judging dimension tend to control schedules, events, and people. Managers scoring high on perceiving tend to control outcomes rather than methods. Both preferences deal with control; judges try to control the environment, while perceivers try to control their participation in the environment and both try to control outcome.

Judging types want a system of order to tackle a project. Perceivers want work that requires change and adaptation. Perceivers are as interested in understanding the job and the process as they are in performing tasks.

Controlling work is a managerial function. Perceivers control the outcome but only a few items of the process. Judges, however, want to control the plan for the process and the outcome. Once judges get their plan organized, it becomes concretized if they don't work at flexibility. If perceivers aren't careful, they will plan too loosely for subordinates to be clear about how the work gets done.

Judging types usually have strong ideas about control and authority. These two variables are givens in a situation. Thus, judge-controllers are usually decisive, fixed, and planned when they begin a task, a project, or a problem. Judge-controllers are outcome-oriented and drive hard to accomplish the plan that will get the desired result.

Perceiving types are more process-oriented, seeing the way a task unfolds as equally important as the outcome. Perceiver managers tend to leave decisions pending while they gather more data. If they aren't careful, they can leave too many things pending and fail to finish projects. Most perceivers take pride in their ability to adapt as they go.

In our work with over 14,000 managers, supervisors, and executives, we found 74% of them to be judge-controllers. Our data shows that judge-controllers were more readily selected for management.

When you look at the managerial functions, you can see that the original way of teaching management appeared to be more natural for judge-controllers. Perceiver-adapters did not appear to have as good a fit. Today, however, adaptability is a primary variable for managers. With fast-paced change, the ability to adapt as you go is essential. Balancing judge-controlling and perceiver-adapting becomes increasingly important.

Judging managers want closure; they want to get things finished. Rarely does a judging manager enjoy the process of doing a project. S/he tends to delay enjoyment until the project is finished. With the focus on the finish instead of the process of doing, the judging manager can develop a driving need to get things finished. When nearing the end of a project, the judging manager can block out all other priorities as the need for release from the project mounts. The need for closure fuels tremendous intensity in the judging manager. This intensity can produce a stubborn or "one-track" pattern as the manager drives toward finishing the project.

The strong judging preference results in wanting to schedule and work according to plan. Preferring advance warning of things to come, the judging manager gets mentally prepared. Let's look at a real situation.

CASE STUDY:
STRONG JUDGE-CONTROLLING

One of our employees is a strong judging type. Lynn scores 47 on judging preference. I try to keep her apprised of future projects so she can mentally start organizing her thoughts on the subject. I never casually mention a project unless I am fairly certain that it will happen. Her judging process is so dominating that once I mention a project, she then holds me accountable. To brainstorm with her, I first let her know ahead of time that I want to brainstorm. I clearly tell her that I have some half-formed thoughts on the subject and just want to chat. I then set a specific time for the brainstorming and remind her during the session that no decisions are being made. Once she focuses on a project idea, she moves it into reality in her mind and begins gearing up to make it happen.

One afternoon her husband stopped by the office. He heard me tell her that I wanted thirty minutes of her time the next day. He chuckled and said, "I see you've learned how to deal with Lynn's need to control things. Even on Saturday she has every minute planned. I finally learned to tell her in the morning if I want her to go jogging with me late that afternoon. That way she is in control of juggling her schedule to make time for the run. I gave up trying to get her to be spontaneous. If I give her a little advance notice, however, she usually rearranges her schedule and then enjoys the change. She's not worth a damn, though, without that advance warning. I worry about her. Our lives are getting more and more complex with the children, our jobs, and our friends. Life is getting harder and harder to predict."

It took some work to identify Lynn's need to control and some negotiation to try to fit her needs into the work pattern of the office. Initially, we irritated each other frequently. Understanding our preferences along the judging and perceiving dimension was the key to building tolerance for differences.

The judging manager wants the essential information of the entire project, even though s/he is responsible for only a small part of the work. The information about the project enables the judging manager to feel more control of his/her part of the work. Controlling, regulating, planning, and deciding are natural dynamics of the judging manager. Order and structure tend to free the judging manager to then react more spontaneously. Judges talk in terms of getting the plan in mind and then "fine-tuning" it. Perceiving managers talk in terms of "hanging loose" to see what's needed.

Just as the judging manager insists on planning ahead, the perceiving manager insists on adapting as you go. Gathering more data and keeping options open are the major themes of the perceiving manager. With high tolerance for ambiguity, the perceiving manager can wait to see what is going to develop since open-endedness is natural.

Early in our work relationship, I failed to use judging-perceiving patterns in my planning. I put Lynn (strong judge-controller) and Alan (strong perceiver-adapter) on the same project. The conflict was immediate. Lynn wanted to analyze all the pieces of the project, assign specific pieces, and set deadlines. Alan was pleasant but noncommital.

Lynn scored 47 as judge-controller and Alan scored 43 as perceiver-adapter. Basic tendencies were 90 points apart. Alan had an intense desire to be independent. He was difficult to pin down. He works best when given enough mental and emotional space to adapt the project as he goes. He is process-oriented and therefore wants the process to be flexible enough to maximize talents and events. Lynn is planning-oriented and therefore wants to control the process from the beginning so she can feel more certain of the success of the results.

Lynn wanted to set regular meetings. Alan wanted to meet as needed. Lynn wanted to set deadlines for each segment of the work. Alan agreed that she could set the deadlines if she wished, but he wouldn't commit to them. Instead of commitment, he responded, "I'll do the best I can." Lynn wanted to do a thorough market search, while Alan wanted to call a few key people in the industry. She wanted to schedule the printers initially; he wanted to wait and see what the project looked like to better determine which printer could best handle the job. The conflicts went on daily.

Putting Alan and Lynn together on that project turned out to be hard on them and time-consuming for me. Much time was needed to help them adjust work patterns, negotiate differences, and build understanding of styles. It took coaching, training, and supervising for the next three projects they worked on together. The reward finally came.

Today they are an excellent team on any project. They reached a point of appreciation for each other's strengths and have come to rely on them. Now they talk openly when they feel irritated over timing, organizing patterns, and different levels of intensity. Changing their individual styles was not the goal. As a manager, I wanted to maximize their individual strengths. My goal was to help them build tolerance and appreciation for different styles. Their acceptance of each other's difference was a bridge to greater understanding of our clients as well, enabling us to respond to client needs more effectively.

Perceiving managers have a need for freedom and independence. Most people do. But for the perceiving manager, freedom and independence are dominant variables in any relationship — whether at work or at home. They like to keep options open, delay decisions, treasure hunt some more, and continue the adventure. Perceivers like to do things at the last minute. Their curiosity fuels their action and adventure drives.

They tend to be rather uninterested in punctuality unless strongly marked by some traumatic event early in life that forced punctuality as an issue. Ordinarily, perceivers see time in terms of opportunity to discover rather than an end in itself. Unlike judges, who see time in terms of decision and therefore control, perceivers prefer to "hang loose" and see what turns up.

When judge-controllers ask someone to go to lunch, they usually select a specific day, time, and location. I jokingly say that judge-controllers write such appointments in their calendars in ink. If perceivers keep a calendar at all, they probably make entries in pencil, preferring to keep options open by erasing pencil entries and putting in more interesting options that turn up at the last minute. Of course, it may not be that extreme, but the point is that judge-controllers organize and schedule and perceivers adapt and wait to see.

Let's review the characteristics:

JUDGE	PERCEIVER
Wants closure	Wants to "hang loose"
Wants to finish	Wants to stay open to something new
Controls time	Controls own participation
Prefers advance notice	Enjoys spontaneous challenges
Likes scheduling and working according to the plan	Likes to start the process and adjust as needed
Likes to do things ahead of time	Likes to do things at the last minute
Prefers decisiveness	Prefers to postpone decisions to see if they really need to be made
Wants only essential information for the plan	Wants ample information to explore more options
Decides and plans	Adapts and changes
Is goal-oriented	Is process-oriented

Can jump to conclusions too quickly just to reduce ambiguity and get closure	Can postpone decisions too long and get pulled in too many directions and be too scattered to decide

Perceivers like change because of the opportunity to adapt; judges fight change until they can get it organized and under control.

The majority of managers and executives we have tested score as judge-controllers. Ninety-three percent (93%) of the organizations we work with are judging-type organizations. In the past, managers were evaluated by judging criteria: planning, organizing, controlling, supervising, and implementing. You probably readily recognize those as major topics in management books and training courses. When the world moved at a slower speed, systems were not as immediately interdependent and the balance of power was easier to identify. Judging managers were preferred. But what about today's unpredictable climate? The management skills that are becoming more valuable are speed, clarity, flexibility, accuracy, and spontaneity — characteristics that tend to be more perceiving than judging.

We are not suggesting that judging characteristics are no longer needed. We are saying that being stuck in a strong preference for one or the other will not be enough to meet today's tough challenges. For years the perceiving manager has been the exception to the norm and has been surrounded by judging managers. Now judging managers have to change old patterns of control and predictability in order to stay abreast of rapidly changing environments. Perceiving managers have to develop more internal order to keep clarity and balance in the data explosion that is hitting them.

CASE STUDY: STRONG
PERCEIVER-ADAPTER PREFERENCE

Randy is the only perceiver-adapter on an executive management team. He is responsible for a highly visible department. It has high customer-interface. His group is responsible for satisfied customers.

Managers reporting to Randy describe him as "laid back unless you really screw up"; "He leaves you alone and lets you do your job"; "He treats you like a professional"; "He is a little too laid back at times. You can't get a decision out of him."

Randy scored 45 as a perceiver-adapter, 41 as a sensor, and 35 as a thinker. He has strong preferences and therefore has fairly predictable patterns since he has seen little reason to develop judge-controlling characteristics. He is an extroverted, personable guy who has appeared to be in the right place at the right time with the right people. He does not appear to be ambitious. He seems much more interested in having enough leisure time than in having status lunches.

For self-starters who know the business, Randy's managerial style leaves them room. He gives general direction, has two clear goals in customer satisfaction, and lets managers run their own show. This approach causes problems, however, with power. When the managers disagree on the way something should be done that affects all of them, Randy just floats along. He avoids clarifying. He just lets problems grow. His refusal to step up to negotiate a solution leaves a vacuum which contributes to power struggles among the managers. Since Randy won't take charge, the managers compete for control.

An ambitious, young professional was hired as a manager in Randy's department. Randy assessed him to be a "go-getter" who would require very little attention to turn into a producer. Randy liked his outgoing personality and thought he had picked a winner.

Instead of helping the new manager become oriented, Randy just left him alone. He assumed the new guy would ask if he wanted to know anything. The new manager scored 45 as a judge-controller. He disliked the loose way things were organized. He wanted to know what his authority was so that he understood clearly where his assignment overlapped other managers and where he was free to act independently. Randy did not provide that clarity and when asked, said he would have to think about it.

The new manager, a super-achiever, was at first annoyed by the lack of direction and deadlines. He asked about an overall plan for customer satisfaction and found the two goals with no plan for implementation. When he realized that no plan had been laid out, he relaxed his irritation with Randy and saw instead a golden opportunity. He studied the market, the competitors, the resources, and designed an ambitious plan for his unit. He was careful to keep a positive relationship with Randy, which wasn't hard to do. Take care of business and Randy would take care of you by not interfering with your plans.

It took the new manager less than a year to absorb most of the power that Randy had abdicated. He was clearly in charge of the department on an informal basis, although Randy still had the formal authority. If you wanted something done in that department, you went to the new manager. Word spread quickly through the organization, and Randy was quietly unseated from his job.

Perceiver-adapting in its balanced form has the flexibility and emergent approach to facilitate dynamic management of a volatile department in an unpredictable market. The ability to "roll with the punches" instead of resisting and trying to control them is an asset in such a job. Letting people have enough freedom to invest ownership in their jobs is a sound principle if it does not become abdication.

JUDGE-PERCEIVER ATTITUDE TOWARD TIME

Perceivers say, "Time is not the goal. Letting life happen is our goal." Judges say, "Time is a valuable asset, not to be wasted."

Perceiver managers tend to be task-oriented instead of time-oriented. How or when the task is accomplished is secondary to the quality of the task. They like to "go with the flow." Their ability to react spontaneously is a strong asset. Therefore, too much controlling and planning short-circuits one of their strengths. One perceiver said, "We control the task and the task controls the employee. We control tasks, not time."

Judge and perceiver managers disagreed strongly on whether or not employees should be punctual. The typical judging position was that time was important and employees dare not abuse it without risking punitive measures. The typical perceiver was flexible on time. A comment that summarized the perceivers' position: "We're not demanding about the time somebody comes to work, if lateness isn't flagrant and they get the job done."

Perceiver managers indicated that they like to keep general time commitments, but liked to retain flexibility. They acknowledged that they frequently underestimated time requirements. Since they did not place a high premium on time, they tended to misuse it.

Judging managers say they watch the clock and work accordingly. They dislike people who waste time. They see time as one of the most valuable resources a person has. They schedule to maximize their time use. Both our behavioral observation research and our statistical data indicate that though judge-controllers greatly value time, they themselves tend not to be punctual. Investigating this phenomena, we found a pattern of judge-controllers trying to finish just one more thing before leaving for a meeting. If ten minutes are available, judge-controllers tend to try to cram something into that time space so they can get closure on one of the many things on their agenda. They therefore tend to overestimate their ability to finish, get caught up in the momentum of closure, and have to rush to the meeting or arrive a few minutes late. The need for closure can override their desire to be punctual.

The following comments from perceiving and judging managers are representative of typical attitudes.

PERCEIVER ATTITUDE TOWARD TIME

"I don't like to be overbooked or overcontrolled. If I get too many things on my calendar, I start to rebel."

"I am resentful of people who are too demanding."

"Overplanning kills my interest. I like adventure and flying by the seat of my pants. It makes me feel alive."

"I like to do what I want to, when I want to. I don't like for someone else to control my time."

"I don't like too much planning or too rigid a filing system. I like to play it loose. Paper is like the bottom of the lake — it will turn up in its own good time."

"I can do last-minute excellence. If I plan too far ahead, I lose the interest and the spontaneity. The quality drops if I plan too far in advance."

"My greatest satisfaction comes from variety."

"If I have to wear a watch, I prefer it to be one with no hands."

JUDGE ATTITUDE TOWARD TIME

"Time is my most valuable resource."

"There is never enough time."

"Time is money."

"I get frustrated because of the inability to control interruptions. I hate the time lost in my momentum for getting things done."

"Anyone who doesn't set priorities and try to stick to them is crazy."

"I hate to be late, but hate even more for others to keep me waiting."

"I prefer deadlines. That allows me to plan accordingly."

"I use 'to-do' lists, both in my head and also on paper."

"I schedule tightly so as not to waste time."

"Those of us who score above 35 on judge-controlling admit that time controls us."

"If I have extra time, I use it to see how many things I can get finished in that time frame."

"I measure my sense of well being in terms of time and getting things done."

"I like to plan everything I do. I occasionally have a 'spell' of spur-of-the-moment things, but I make a conscious decision to allow myself to be spontaneous. Otherwise, I can't do it."

That last comment highlights the natural preference of judging that has to consciously decide to use the skill of perceiving-adapting. Our natural preference is easier to use than its counterpart.

Judges like to live in a planned, orderly way as they try to control and regulate life. Perceivers like to live in adaptable, spontaneous ways as they try to understand and savor life.

PERCEIVER ATTITUDE TOWARD PLANNING

"Planning in general is necessary, but not too specific. General direction is fine, but not details."

"Task deadlines determine the plan. I don't have to spend much time on that."

"If you control time by planning tasks, then you don't have to watch the clock or the people."

"If you are liberal with your people about time, but plan the tasks, they will usually give you more than you ask."

"Much of my plan stays in my head. I don't see much need to commit it to paper. It's just a general outline anyway."

"We are extremely high producers or we don't work at all. We just don't have the intensity that judge-controllers have."

"We like to do things at the last minute. If we miss a deadline, we can usually adjust."

"I hate my calendar. I use a little daily calendar. I just can't tolerate one of those big ones that tries to define you for a year."

"I prioritize in my mind according to the day's dictation. That way, I can adjust without changing paperwork."

"I like doing things spontaneously . . . working under pressure is joyous."

"If I agree to something too far in the future, it begins to nag at me and makes me feel committed . . . I may back out at the last minute . . . I just don't like to plan too far ahead. I'm that way away from work too. I hate to get tickets ahead of time."

Perceiver-adapters just don't want too much structure. Freedom to respond is more important. They like to "hang loose."

JUDGE ATTITUDE TOWARD PLANNING

"Planning is an absolute requirement."

"Prioritizing ahead of time gives the best utilization of resources."

"Planning provides confidence that we know where we are going and sets a clear direction."

"Planning helps determine adequacy of performance."

"Planning helps identify short- and long-term goals."

"Comprehensibility and flexibility come as a result of good planning."

"I can be spontaneous just as soon as I get organized."

"Planning is a means to reduce stress levels."

"The point of life is the end result . . . the finishing of something brings the satisfaction."

"Purposeful planning avoids wasted time."

"I don't like surprises. I want even movement. Abrupt changes annoy me because there isn't time to plan. I like to have input into changes."

"I am determined to get it done."

You can see the clear theme of order, control, and authority running through the comments.

PERCEIVER ATTITUDE TOWARD CONTROL

"We don't like to control the small stuff. We don't care to. We are interested in controlling the big stuff."

"I don't like to make all the decisions."

"If you take on the decision, you take on the responsibility and can get weighed down with the responsibility. I don't like the entanglement."

"We don't like to make all the decisions. Too much responsibility. We frequently experience post-decision regret. We usually second-guess our decisions if they are truly important."

"We are most receptive to gentle persuasion. We do not like to be controlled, so we figure that others are the same. If it's too slick, I really resent it."

JUDGE ATTITUDE TOWARD CONTROL

"I like to know clearly the parameters. I want to know the limits, guidelines, boundaries, security . . . There is anarchy without it. With clear parameters, individual flexibility makes sense."

"By the time I hear the information, I start to make decisions; sometimes I don't even wait to hear all of the details."

"I like to be in control, but if I really need it, I will turn to someone for support and help rather than face the possibility of getting out of control."

"We push, drive, direct, and advise in order to get things done according to our plan. We are critical and opinionated about the way things and people should work."

"I want authority and power — that saves my sanity because it allows me to have order and predictability."

One of the most striking differences between judge and perceiver attitudes is seen in the following comments. A perceiver said, "Work should be play; so I make my work playful." A judge-controller countered: "Work should be finished first and then, if there is time, we can play."

BALANCE BETWEEN JUDGE-CONTROLLING AND PERCEIVER-ADAPTING

The perceptive attitude focuses on incoming data. Curiosity, spontaneity, enthusiasm, and adventure characterize this preference. The judging attitude focuses on decision, closure, planning, organizing, and controlling.

The need for balance is well stated by Briggs and McCaulley:

"Procrastination comes from perception with a deficit of judgment. Prejudice comes from judgment with a deficit of perception." (p. 14)

Balancing the perceptive and judging processes is critical to leadership. You have seen how the perceptive attitude allows adaptability that is required today, as I am sure you see the planning skill so representative of judge-controllers. We are suggesting that a good decision requires that you use both.

When you make a decision, careful attention to each process should give you a thorough grasp of the decision and its possibilities for acceptance. Try thorough and systematic use of each process.

1. Use sensory-perception to assess the facts. See the reality of the situation. Observe what is actually happening in the present. Note what people are saying and doing, what is happening in the environment, what are the physical factors in the external world affecting the situation.

2. Use feeler-judgment to feel people's positions, involvement, prejudices, commitments, and reactions to the situation. Try to see your own reactions to the situation. See and feel the degree of agreeableness or disagreeableness in your reaction . . . then see other people's responses. Consider personal values and concerns as you add this to your sensory assessment of facts.

3. Use thinker-judgment to develop a rationale. Try to determine cause and effect. Establish the principal variables involved. Clearly state the problem, explore alternatives, develop your rationale, and look at consequences of various decisions. Include both sensory facts and feeler judgment in your rationale.

4. Use intuitive-perception to explore implications of your alternatives, to identify relationships, and intuit outcomes. Explore innovative ways of seeing the situation. Search out possibilities.

Begin with facts, explore values, analyze cause and effect, and identify implications. Balance on judge and perceiving is essential to effective decision-making.

Too much reliance on judging preference produces such control and rigidity that the total picture doesn't evolve. Too much reliance on perceiving preference produces such adaptability that the total picture doesn't become ordered. Both are needed to make the whole.

— 7 —

Organizational
and Managerial Style

If a typology is useful in identifying habitual patterns of human behavior, then it should also be useful in identifying patterns of organizations. We found the Myers-Briggs to be a useful typology for both individuals and organizations.

David Keirsey and Marilyn Bates provided an excellent framework for organizational insight in their book *Please Understand Me*. Their work in 1978 provided a paradigm for organizational observation that we find continually useful. Isabel Briggs-Myers and Mary McCaulley's *Manual: A Guide to the Development and Use of the Myers-Briggs Type Indicator* provides the other research foundation that is invaluable in understanding organizational dynamics.

We find that the majority of organizations with which we work are principally STJ organizations (sensing, thinking, judging). Regardless of the mission statement, the militaristic or athletic model still predominates. We read about unique organizational approaches that are highlighted in popular management literature, but we find the majority of people still working in more traditional organizational structures. Even organizations which do not function from the STJ model initially tend to move in that direction as they reach a certain level of growth. The larger the organization, the more it tends to become bureaucratic.

146

STJ ORGANIZATIONS
(SENSOR, THINKER, JUDGE)

The theme of the STJ organization is *hierarchy*. Titles mean something. Authority, title, and status delineate the structure around which other dynamics move. Principal beliefs of a hierarchical organization are:

Respect your boss.
Observe the chain of command.
Follow standard operating procedures.
Control decisions and interactions by policy and procedure.
Pay your dues before you move up the hierarchy.
Take only carefully calculated risks within the structure.
Make your contributions clearly measurable in a competitive area.

Just describing the STJ characteristics makes the organization look ill-suited to deal with today's volatile environment. The STJ organization is traditionalist, with strong values of conservatism and stabilization. With change and unpredictability, we have to question the survivability of the STJ organization if productivity and cost-effectiveness is the measure.

STJ Managerial Role

The management role in the STJ organization is usually seen as a dominant controller of work. Emphasizing work roles rather than the worker is part of the hierarchical theme. The focus is on the work and the roles required to complete the work. Individuals are not valued as much as the role they play in work accomplishment.

Fast-track managers are usually identified because of their tough-minded ability to get others to do the job. STJ organizational hierarchy favors employees for their loyalty, responsibility, and industriousness. They prefer down-to-earth, economical solutions and fast turnaround.

Dominant STJ managers within an STJ organization are continually reinforced and frequently rewarded for the way they work. They appear to fit naturally with organizational norms. STJ managers are usually impatient with anyone failing to comply with the STJ standards of work. They tend to support the following standards:

Use standard operating procedures — "That's what they're there for!"

Play by the rules — "People who don't, can't be trusted."

Meet deadlines — "People who miss deadlines aren't good workers."

Get to work on time — "We have rules about starting and stopping."

Be realistic — "Make it down-to-earth . . . give us something we can use. Don't ask us to guess or estimate."

Accomplish tasks — "We're here to work, not to sit around talking about work. Don't waste time."

Work can be measured — "Talking, thinking, and meetings aren't as important as the work you can do with your hands."

Honor chain of command — "Protect your boss . . . respect the position."

Follow procedure — "It is necessary to get things done."

STJ managers can annoy other people by too strictly adhering to rules. STJ managers want people to be loyal to them and to the organization. They measure loyalty principally by how well employees adhere to their standards of work. They are usually intolerant of anyone who does not accept the organization or who is too challenging about the way things are done. They like workers who do their work the way the boss wants.

STJ managers may be seen by others as pessimistic, critical, sarcastic, stubborn drivers of the organization. The very characteristics that provide STJ managers the ability to stick to the job until it is finished may contribute to the perception that they are so task-driven that they may not be tolerant of anyone who sees the organization or tasks differently. Scoring as an STJ manager is not proof that these negative characteristics are part of your management style. They do suggest that you have a propensity for those characteristics unless you have consciously chosen to balance them. On a tired day or a day when you are not as disciplined as usual, your chances of showing those characteristics will be greater.

Typical weaknesses of the STJ manager are impatience, resistance to change, and negativity. A manager with STJ preferences is usually reluctant to change priorities. Once the plan is organized, the manager is usually irritated at changes in the plan — particularly changes that someone else imposes. The STJ manager is usually impatient when projects or tasks get delayed. If the impatience is too great, it will impede the problem-solving process to get the project back on track. The impatience can turn into anger at people instead of clearly focusing on the problem. STJ managers tend to look for the people causing the problem rather than looking to see if the work process itself is causing dysfunctional flow of work.

STJ managers can become overly concerned with negative possibilities and develop a pattern of wasting energy in excessive worry about the work. The more worried STJs become, the more controlling they become. Anxiety can then affect decision-making capacity by freezing creative problem-solving energies. They can decide the issue too quickly just to relieve the pressure. They can settle for a "make-do" decision rather than a problem-solving solution.

In the past, STJ managers and STJ organizations appeared to work well in a more stable world that operated at a slower pace. But things are changing at a rapid pace. We are *not* saying that STJ managers are obsolete. We are saying that each set of preferences has its set of negative possibilities. Anyone who gets stuck in a set of preferences without thorough development of alternative skills will find her/himself in dysfunctional managerial form. The danger of a managerial style being reinforced by the same organizational structure is the false encouragement to the manager to be satisfied with his/her style. Being stuck in STJ preferences will not be enough for the challenge.

We encourage you to again consider our assertion: TO BE A LEADER, ONE MUST DO ONGOING, THOROUGH, BRUTAL SELF-EXAMINATION. When the fit is too good between the manager and organizational style, the incentive to self-examine is considerably lessened. Being too comfortable can easily lead to complacency. We have evidence in our leadership studies that balanced development on the four dimensions is essential for leadership. A manager can only become a long-term leader if s/he develops the potential of all eight possibilities by maximizing the strengths of extroversion and introversion, sensing and intuiting, thinking and feeling, and judging and perceiving. Managers can have strong preferences and undeveloped alternative styles. Leaders cannot afford that luxury.

STJ managers tend to weigh facts of the moment more heavily in making decisions than possible impact of that decision. They tend to have less interest in the long-term effect of the decision.

They are most reactive to current stimuli and less impressed with possible future implications of the information. This tendency reinforces their preference for facts in making decisions. They tend to undervalue information about the way their decision affects others. They tend to make the assumption that work is more important than the people who do the work. STJ managers like to decide things quickly, implement decisions, and move on to other challenges.

STJ managers like to schedule and order things. They don't want to be caught unprepared. They dislike last-minute changes of schedule and can be quite rigid about their plans. They usually value promptness and dislike waiting. Let's look at an example of these patterns.

Case Study: An STJ Manager

Dan is an STJ engineer in an STJ-dominant organization. He scored 45 as a sensor, 53 as a thinker, and 49 as a judge. He has very strong preferences on each dimension, and his fast rise in the organization reinforced those patterns. Since promotions came fast and his success was measurable, Dan was certain that his style was excellent.

When our firm first began working with the management team of his company, Dan was one of the most arrogant and abusive managers. He was a thirty-one-year-old superstar with an air of self-importance that permeated all interactions. His mentor had given him larger and larger challenges, and each time. Dan had produced. Few people took the time to look at the devastation he left behind, but the projects were completed. Since his mentor looked at the bottom line, the hierarchical structure supported his results and didn't track the method of the results.

Dan moved right up the ladder with little thought about his impact on people. He was focused on getting the job done. He just assumed that using people was part of organizational practice. He failed to see the difference between "using people" and "working with people."

We were facilitating a planning retreat for the management group. Two hours into the session, Dan had already been asserting his domination of the group. In the small group sessions he had talked to other group members using the following statements: "That's stupid"; "You're full of bullshit"; "You don't know what you're talking about"; and "Don't waste my time with your elementary ideas." By the end of the first day, Dan had repeated his patterns of domination, criticism, and analytical arrogance.

After the retreat he asked me to give him my opinion of the group. That was just the opening I had been waiting for. I described clearly the methods he had used to intimidate and control group interaction. I cited specific behaviors, phrases he used, techniques he used to end discussion when someone had a valid point he could not refute. He used a combination of insult, innuendo, and intellectually confusing terms to stump people who tried to oppose his point of view. I expected an attack. Instead, Dan appeared to be listening intently. He asked two questions. We discussed those, but he dropped his argumentative approach and was using a conversational tone. He abruptly closed our discussion with "I don't think I agree with you, but I will think it over."

Over the next two years we continued to work with the management group as needed. Our specific assignment was to facilitate communication and clarity among group members. Over time, Dan modified his style a bit, but he didn't really see a need to develop intuitive insight into his pattern of behavior. He was not convinced that he needed to be more sensitive to people's feelings and saw no need to be more flexible. Things were going his way. His preferred patterns appeared to be getting him what he wanted.

A promotion, however, jarred him so that he began to question his own style. He was promoted to executive vice-president and moved into a situation where his success depended upon a number of division heads. Previously, he was in control of one division located at one site. Now he could no longer dominate on a day-to-day basis since the divisions were scattered throughout seven states. He recognized that he was now more dependent upon people at the various sites. His old pattern of dominating and interrogating was dependent upon his ability to maintain surveillance. His new situation made that impossible. He couldn't be present continuously to force their compliance. His old methods clearly didn't work in the new situation. Suddenly, he felt vulnerable.

During the first six months on the job, Dan tripled the paperwork of the division heads at each location. He tried to devise report forms that would allow him to control what was happening at each site. He finally realized that reports would not give him the kind of control he was accustomed to having. Surprise visits to the locations didn't seem to work either, since the grapevine carried the alert if he left his office.

Dan's stress level became so high that his body finally told him that something was seriously wrong. His style was no longer adequate for the new job. The new job was more abstract, complex, unpredictable, and certainly less controllable than any assignment he had had in the past. He disliked the idea that he was dependent on people whom he could not find a way to force into compliance.

Dan came face-to-face with an overpowering fear of failure. In his meteoric career he had known continual success. At this point, he was facing mid-thirties and had never failed professionally. He liked the power and prestige of success and was surprised to realize he desperately needed it. He discovered that he was terrified of failure and disgrace. An important part of the training for leadership was missing: an understanding of failure that comes through experiencing it. An intellectual understanding of the concept is not enough. Until he has failed and come to know those energies and the defeating thoughts and feelings that accompany failure, he can't really wear a long-term leadership hat.

Until he could see that his favorite style was defeating him, Dan did not know what a tremendous fear of failure was driving him. His arrogant intolerance of anyone else's failure was an indicator of his immaturity on the subject.

Our world is organized around the concept of duality. To be wise, the leader must know success and failure, power and powerlessness, winning and losing. Dan's behavior did not indicate that he had experience on both sides of the coin. How could he then have wisdom to understand? His harsh judgment of anyone who "messed up" hinted at the amount of energy he used to keep his own fear of failure suppressed.

His current position helped to push that fear into consciousness as he realized that his old methods were not working. In six months he developed high blood pressure, gained twenty-five pounds, drank excessively, and experienced sexual dysfunction. Dan's physical system was bearing the brunt of his desperate need to control in order to avoid failure.

He gave us a call and asked us to come and work with him on a managerial plan. He said, "I think I'm ready to quit arguing with you on the people perspective. Let's get started. I don't know what to do first, but I do know I have to do something different. We are facing too many crises and we've got to form a tighter team or we might not make it."

We began to systematically reexamine his managerial systems from the checkpoints of balancing his judge-controlling tendencies with perceiver-adapting skills, sensing facts with intuitive implications, thinking analysis with feeling awareness, and introverting privacy with extroverting group process.

He wanted the managers reporting to him to do a better job of developing the skills of their employees also. He knew that people could give them the competitive edge in an increasingly difficult market.

We could have chosen another strategy for Dan and his group. We chose the Myers-Briggs to establish a common language by which we could talk about the "ambiguous" side of management — the people side. We were working with Dan's style as a principal intervention. He was the dominant person in the hierarchy and was finely attuned to hierarchical structure. He recognized that his job had become more complex and more unpredictable, and that the structure must be tempered with creative, adaptive systems. If the STJ manager at the top of an STJ organization wants a different use of power for the organization, then the top manager must set the pace.

We don't overlook the fact that Dan's preference for control has not changed; he is balancing that preference by developing better people skills, sharing decision-making authority where feasible, and giving people more freedom in the way they meet corporate goals. By rethinking his own style, he is also redesigning his reporting system. He had to come up with a better way to determine the work of each division.

Previously, his sensor-thinker preferences were demanding voluminous fact and rationale reports. Now he is thinking in a more intuitive way. He has identified the critical parts of the job and uses targeted control data. He has taken an overview of the work and identified the non-negotiable parts of division work that must be done well. He is working with the principle that a report generated for his office must also be useful to the division. That principle is requiring him to work with division heads to help them think more clearly about the information they need to more effectively manage. He is on his way toward long-term productive leadership. He is finding ways to develop people and himself.

A critical turn in Dan's development came with his recognition and admission of his fear of failing. By admitting the fear and turning to face it, he began the arduous task of conquering it. As he developed more of his least preferred characteristics, he began moving toward being more clear, more unlimited, more wise, and more courageous than he was when he was pridefully stuck in strong preferences.

NTJ ORGANIZATIONS
(INTUITOR, THINKER, JUDGE)

Another type of organization that we encounter is an NTJ-dominant organization; however, we find more NTJ upper-level executives than we find NTJ organizations. The majority of organizations that we work with are still STJ-dominant organizations, even though top leadership may have an NTJ preference. The larger the organization, the greater the need for STJ reliance on standard operating procedures, chain of command, and multiple policies and rules.

An NTJ organization is continually innovating. The driving theme is *improvement.* This type of organization values originality, creativity, and new ways of doing things. The mission is more important than anything else. Mission is the prime decision variable, superseding individuals, departments, and programs. The NTJ organization is driven by a vision of the ideal system and seeks continuously to develop prototypes, pilots, and models throughout the organization that are conceptually harmonious with that vision.

One architectural firm has a mission motto: "We help shape tomorrow." That motto was the guideline for judging projects. They used creativity, uniqueness, applicability, and status as their criteria. Though you may find those abstract terms difficult to accept as criteria, they were nevertheless used mercilessly in reviewing ideas and projects. Anything that seemed ordinary, redundant, or too traditional was rejected.

The NTJ organization drives itself to grow and develop. The organization must be creative in its effort to maintain a leading edge in innovative programming. It does continuous planning for organizational change to meet future needs. This type organization is finding itself well suited to today's ambiguous business climate.

NTJ Managerial Role

The management role of the NTJ is largely visionary. With the continual striving for improvement, the NTJ feels an intensity to be unique. Driven by the need for individuality, the NTJ manager can get trapped in the search for uniqueness and lose touch with the practical aspects of doing business.

The intuitive preference focuses on innovative approaches to tomorrow. It involves changing methods and adapting patterns to create unusual effects. This dynamic preference, however, when matched with strong judging preference can limit the creative nature and put it under such rigid judgment that it may cease to function well. The intuitive, thinker, judge frequently finds the demon master within. Since the high standards and desire for designing the superior model is self-motivated, the NTJ can be a relentless and heartless task master. The NTJ is usually more harsh in self-judgment than in judging others.

NTJ managers can set such high standards, however, that employees may feel that it is impossible to reach them. No matter how hard they work or how well they prepare, NTJ managers can find several ways to improve their performance. The search for improvement is perpetual.

NTJ managers tend to be quite impatient with those who do not strive for their high standards of innovation and excellence. They tend to value originality, intelligence, perceptive insights, progressive ideas, and innovative approaches. They tend to be impatient with irrational actions, standard operating procedures, anything ordinary, laziness, slow progress, errors, and failure to learn from errors. NTJ managers are annoyed by cliches, shallow thinking, and traditional approaches to problem-solving. In short, NTJ managers are most attracted to other NTs. Other types just don't seem to be as intensely focused on innovative improvement.

Perhaps you noticed how judgmental the NTJs seem to be. The intuitive nature demands innovative complexity; the analytical nature demands logical actions; and the judgmental nature demands efficiency and effectiveness. It is most difficult for an NTJ to live up to his/her own expectations; others find it almost impossible.

NTJ managers tend to make critical observations at inappropriate times. Although the criticism is usually valid, the timing is often wrong. I observed one NTJ manager whose timing was bad.

Case Study: An NTJ Manager

Andy is a sensitive, creative young man. He is dedicated to his manager and to doing an excellent job. He approached the manager full of excitement about an interaction he had just had with a group of design engineers. He joyfully shared with his manager the issues discussed, his strategy, and his interactions that secured their agreement. He was glowing with the joy of winning. Just at that moment the NTJ manager said, "Looks like you did a good job, Andy, but you'd better get back with them and nail down those target dates. You probably should have done that at the time. You sometimes get so excited you miss some of the minor things. But overall, you did a good job."

As I watched the interaction, I saw Andy visibly slump and the joy of the interaction faded quickly. He heard his boss's comments as statements of fault rather than minor adjustments to the successful negotiation.

You may be thinking that Andy was just too sensitive. Before you accept that reasoning, look again at the people dynamics. Andy was sharing his winning with the boss. He was not asking for his opinion; he was asking for his appreciation and approval. The NTJ boss misread the cue or ignored it and gave instead advice and rejection of the win.

As the NTJ boss and I walked away from the crestfallen Andy, the boss said, "What did I say? Andy seemed to be upset about something." That remark gave me opportunity to discuss his sense of timing. I asked him if any harm would have been done if Andy had been allowed to savor his win and then a bit later discuss the minor corrections. By delaying the "perceived criticism" until the joy of winning had been thoroughly experienced, Andy's receptivity would probably have been greater. You may think that a busy manager doesn't have time to get back but must capture the moment. I say a busy manager must keep employee motivation in mind continually.

The NTJ boss said, "You know, I make that same mistake with my wife and my kids. I just assume that when they tell me something, they want my opinion about it. It didn't occur to me that they could really mean 'tell me that you like me.' I wish people would say what they mean." NTJ managers frequently mistake appreciation cues for advice-seeking cues, thereby hurting feelings when others needed appreciation rather than "criticism."

NTJ managers tend to ask questions that sound judgmental instead of information-seeking. Too frequently, they phrase questions beginning with "Why didn't you . . ." instead of "Tell me about . . ." The probing questions of the NTJ are indicative of high expectations they have for themselves and others. This critical demand for excellence can make employees feel powerless to ever truly please the NTJ manager.

Some NTJ managers have worked hard to develop their sensing, feeling, perceiving skills and are developing a more balanced approach. However, the tendency to continually escalate standards in the ongoing struggle to improve things can demoralize others. NTJs are impatient with human error and move quickly to correct things and people; the struggle to remain sensitive and patient is a mighty challenge.

The NTJ has great strength in the ability to stand alone and move toward a vision. This strength can easily become weakness when the NTJ loses the ability to objectively interpret data that challenges that vision. At some point the NTJ can become so committed to his/her own vision that ability to objectively interpret "negative" data fades. When the vision is perceived by the NTJ to be ethically and rationally correct, s/he may not seek input. Thus, the brilliance or the inappropriateness of the vision can be extreme. NTJs tend to have great losses and/or great wins. The key is the ability to realistically interpret data involving the vision. Clear, brutal self-examination of perception is essential.

NF MANAGERIAL ROLE
(INTUITOR, FEELER)

Since we find few NF organizations, we will focus on the NF manager. The NF manager is driven by the need for personal growth. The intuitive drive for the perfect model and feeling sensitivity combine to create a strong impetus toward personal and organizational growth. The NF manager wants people to be cooperative, harmonious, and self-determined.

NF managers play the roles of catalysts or energizers. They tend to avoid supervision since they prefer decisions by participation and workers who are self-motivated. Although they have strong ideas about how people should perform, they frequently feel irritated when they actually have to correct someone's performance. They have strong ideas about how people *should* behave. The NFs tend to avoid confrontation and may feel resultant anger at those who don't behave as they should. Since harmony is the primary goal of the NF, confrontation may be seen as bad and anyone causing the confrontation as unlikeable. NFs try to select staff who are self-starters to minimize their supervising job and reduce the potential for confrontation.

The NF manager is usually persuasive and convinces people to do their jobs through a mixture of enthusiasm, acceptance, and warmth. By setting up the expectation of enthusiastic acceptance, the NF may hurt people's feelings when under pressure. When they get too stressed, NFs may abort their participative decision-making style and issue harsh, authoritative decisions. This action takes employees by surprise; they may feel manipulated and possibly betrayed. The need for reducing their own anxieties may temporarily override NF preference for harmony and group participation.

NF managers typically are annoyed by insensitive people, unkind remarks, lack of appreciation, and emotionally cold workplaces. They dislike rudeness, conflict, and people who aren't team players.

They tend to annoy others by introducing emotional issues. They will probably take moralistic and/or emotional stands on issues and can usually get people stirred up over issues. Sometimes they argue the morality of an issue and become so embroiled that they incorrectly identify the problem. They tend to smooth over rather than address problems.

Well-balanced NFs are among the most charming and charismatic types. Their warm appreciation of people and their sensitivity has a strong attracting quality. They have abilities to build teamwork environments and create shared responsibility in the work.

Case Study: An NFJ Manager

Jim is an NFJ division head of a large state social service agency. The mission of the agency is to help poor people. At first glance you might assume that an intuitive feeler would be a good fit with a helping agency. The truth, however, is that the bureaucratic organization was strongly STJ (sensor, thinker, judge).

Jim had 550 people in his division. His goals were still individual growth for all employees and the division. He wanted his division to be responsive and genuinely devoted to helping people. The rules and regulations from both state and federal levels, however, made this goal difficult to reach.

As Jim became more and more burdened by the irrationality and insensitivity of the system, he turned to his management staff for stronger support. He became less tolerant of complaints from the field. Although he asked a group of case workers from across the division to meet with him monthly to help him keep in touch, it soon became evident that Jim became visibly upset when they shared problems with him. He interpreted problems as complaints.

When one of the case workers, new to the group, suggested that the reporting form on nutrition was obsolete, Jim responded angrily: "Maybe you had better hold your opinion until you've been around longer. You don't even know the history of that form. I helped develop it myself and I can assure you we use every bit of that information."

Quickly, the word passed that the monthly sessions were "rah-rah" sessions, and smart case workers had better play the game.

Two of the management staff observed Jim's increasing defensiveness and tried to discuss it with him. He sullenly listened to them, thanked them, and courteously showed them to the door. He privately labeled them as having bad attitudes. He favored "team" players. Unfortunately, he was so stressed and stuck in his preferences that his idea of a team player had come to mean a person who told him what he wanted to hear. Truth had little relevance at this point.

In the midst of this burn-out phase, where Jim became more and more feeling and judgmental and less capable of clearly interpreting information, he hired a controller from private industry. The controller, a manipulative boss-pleaser, in a short time convinced Jim that he was one of the few loyal people on the team. The controller focused his energy on making Jim feel good and skillfully created doubt about other members of the group.

Fortunately, Jim's wife is an astute observer and knows her husband very well. She realized that Jim was bitterly complaining about people whom he had formerly valued. She recognized the hardening of perception and insisted that he talk to someone who could help him understand what was going on. In only two sessions, Jim's perception cleared and he got back in touch with his analytical thinking skills and his ability to accurately read sensory data. He began to balance quickly. He saw the manipulative patterns of the boss-pleaser and moved to correct the model he had been setting among his employees.

We do not suggest that the Myers-Briggs is a curative instrument. We are saying that busy, bright, hard-working people can get sidetracked. It is difficult to stay clear and use all eight areas in a balanced way.

Jim changed a number of things he was doing. He changed some of his work habits, built in more time for moving around the building to chat with people informally, and got back in touch with people. He developed a stress management plan, working with nutrition, exercise, and his guitar. He worked on balancing himself physically, emotionally, and mentally.

STP MANAGERIAL ROLE
(SENSOR, THINKER, PERCEIVER)

We rarely find STP managers in executive positions. We find them in supervisory positions but rarely find at the top. The strong need for freedom and independence of the STP is usually thwarted by the complex forces in executive management. Please note: we are not saying STP managers can't handle executive positions. We are saying that they do not appear to *want* the positions. The STP manager likes to deal with expedient needs of the situation; therefore, STPs find forecasting, planning, strategizing, investing, and long-range planning dull and cumbersome. Supervisory interaction with people and work tends to be more satisfying to the STP.

The STP tends to prefer roles of negotiator or troubleshooter where s/he can move in quickly, respond spontaneously, and move on to the next problem. The troubleshooter role is generally more appealing than a managerial role. Action and movement are more appealing to STPs than paperwork, procedure, planning, controlling, and meetings. STPs tend to choose action over ideation, lightness over seriousness, and cleverness over sameness.

An STP who chooses to accept a managerial role tends to approach the job nontraditionally. We have observed a tendency to manage as a troubleshooter rather than daily supervising agent. Troubleshooting seems to be a natural fit for the STP. With sensory capacity to realistically assess the situation and the perceiver enjoyment of spontaneous reaction, the STP plunges into the situation. Very much like an athlete getting "energy up for the game," the STP manager finds inner resources energized in a situation requiring quick response.

As a reactor more than an initiator, the STP frequently waits for external trouble before taking charge. Action and impulsivity are strong preferences. Process is more important to them than product. Rarely have we seen an STP micro-manage. It seems to have little appeal. They are interested in the outcome but don't seem to need or want to control the day-to-day tasks that lead to outcome.

One STP manager told us, "Rules and regulations were designed for no other reason than to irritate. All they are good for is to restrict real work and real fun." Restrictions, rules, and too much supervision are burdensome realities to the STP. S/he dislikes standard operating procedures, while much preferring flexibility and freedom to develop the work method during the process.

Too much talk without enough action is sure to irritate the STP. Boredom is to be avoided and action is the antidote. "Work should be fun and interesting," says the STP. S/he prefers realism instead of speculation, flexibility instead of rigidity, openness instead of rehearsal, cleverness instead of repetitiveness, freedom instead of restrictions, and fun instead of seriousness.

Case Study: An STP Manager

Ben is such a "laid back" guy, you might walk right past him and never suspect that he is deputy director of a large agency. He radiates good humor and a sense of fun. One day he will be impeccably dressed with conservative suit and superb accessories; the very next day he might wear an outlandish tie over a cherry-pink shirt under a bold, plaid jacket. A sense of merriment permeates his office as he delightedly watches people's responses.

Ben is very intelligent and encourages the people in the department to do excellent work. He personally dislikes detailed work and boring procedures, but carefully hires people who are good at that. He spends most of his time moving around the organization, talking to people, joking, and creating a sense of camaraderie.

Ben's secretary, an STJ (sensor, thinker, judge), said, "He is so spontaneous, he nearly drives me crazy. Instead of organizing his work, he works on whatever takes his attention. He calls me into his office a dozen times a day to dictate letters. Instead of doing the mail at one sitting, he works on it off and on throughout the day. If he weren't such a good guy, I would not be able to stand it here.''

Two of the department heads got into a power struggle. They began withholding information critical to each other's work. Ben heard rumors about the conflict but didn't take it seriously. The situation became volatile before he paid much attention. When he realized that it was serious, he went to each department head individually. He carefully listened to each perspective, identifying major issues, errors in perception, and irritations.

When he finished the preliminary work, he took the two men to lunch. He was in a marvelous mood, full of fun and stories. Both department heads were anxiously awaiting the confrontation. Ben appeared to be oblivious of their concern. His own good humor gradually reduced their tension. As they drove back to the office, Ben continued to chat about sports and politics. Just as they stepped into the office building and started toward their separate offices, Ben said, "Let's go down to my office and get you two guys straightened out."

Just as the two thought they had slipped past a confrontation, Ben surprised them by identifying their problem and giving an order to resolve it. Ben has a sense of timing and positivity that makes him an excellent troubleshooter.

Ben is a typical STP in his sense of enjoyment. Judge-controllers usually have difficulty with the STP ability to take events less seriously. Their "go-with-the-flow" approach is almost unfathomable to a strong judging type. Ben frequently misses deadlines, unless they are critical to his survival. Deadlines just don't hold his attention. He has been wise enough to hire an excellent secretary who does follow through. Likewise, his department heads carry the ball for him. They have come to respect his political savvy and his people network. Over time, the department heads have come to accept his strengths and they are the balance for his weaknesses, since they systematically do the work.

Ben gives others little advance warning about projects. His dislike of planning and forecasting is hard on others, making it difficult for them to plan their work. Ben frequently overrides established priorities and redirects people. At times this is necessary, but most often it results from his boredom. He refuses to discipline his own restlessness in order to facilitate the productivity of the group. His unpredictability causes problems for the staff.

The STP manager loves risk and spontaneity so much that organizing and planning just don't get much attention — unless there is conscious discipline of those tendencies.

Ben relies on his strengths but refuses to do the difficult work of developing balancing skills for his weak areas.

SUMMARY

Comparing the four types of managerial patterns is useful in identifying work patterns in organizations. Each pattern has strengths and weaknesses. The stronger plan is to adapt the managerial style to the situation. Balance among the preferences gives the individual more flexibility to adapt to the situation.

Organizational cultures are changing, and leaders are needed to focus the changes.

— 8 —

Leadership
and People Savvy

Accepting a challenge and assessing necessary resources to meet the challenge are inextricably linked. Is it not also reasonable to identify the personal resources needed to accept the challenge of leadership? A personal style inventory, like the Myers-Briggs, is a useful way to personally assess where you are and what you want to develop.

The challenges today force us to change and to grow. In the rush to compete in the marketplace and the management suite, we have too often overlooked the personal style of the individual. We've focused on advanced techniques, strategies, and technologies, but still seem to be rather puzzled by people. We can no longer overlook the people element with the arrogant judgment that there is no scientifically quantifiable way to read people. We have to risk our perceptive abilities to read people since formulas don't work. We have to learn to see, to hear, and to recognize a person's habitual ways of communicating, processing information, judging, and controlling. We assert that the patterns exist; skilled reading of those patterns can be learned.

Leaders must be excellent readers of people. They must read themselves as accurately and objectively as they read others. They must read change and continue their own internal growth and expansion to meet the challenge.

INEVITABLE CHANGE

Since Alvin Toffler so eloquently framed the changes in the twentieth and twenty-first centuries, many people have become focused on trends. Trying to articulate those trends has become big business. Carolyn Corbin summarizes those changes:

> There has been a shift in cultural dominance of major institutions from the past to the present. During the First Wave, the major institution was the family. During the Second Wave, the major institutions were the corporation and the government. And in the New Age Economy, the major institution will be the individual. The major emphasis in the New Age Economy will be on individual, or self-fulfillment. (p. 29)
>
> No longer will there be a we-they attitude among employees and management; a team approach will ensue because of the need to share information and work in order to get the job accomplished. (p. 32, *Strategies 2000*)

If the prediction on self-fulfillment is accurate, the resistance to old management approaches will increase. The traditional use of power and authority will be steadily resisted and challenged. The traditional approach to management will be more and more difficult. Old patterns of issuing orders and expecting compliance will be continually thwarted.

> Shifting demographics, especially the large, aggressive baby boom generation, has changed both the productivity and philosophy of the labor force . . . By 1990, the baby boomers will account for 54% of all workers. Being accustomed to making demands and creating changes, baby boomers will want to stress experiential process of work equal to the material rewards of the career. Loyalty to corporations will continue to decrease because baby boomers have always been self-dependent and oriented to self-fulfillment. Turnover in the labor force will continue to proliferate. Total devotion to job will decline as they pursue interests outside the corporation. (p. 33, *Strategies 2000*)

Workers want more satisfaction on the job. Does it not also reasonably follow that they will demand more from those in charge? How can you respond to workers' satisfaction without dynamic leadership? Baby boomers tend to value experiencing something as well as having traditional status toys. They want to experience the world. Thus, anyone attempting to be a leader must have rich internal experience of who and what the human being is capable of becoming. It may be that today's leader will have to be as capable of demonstrating continual evolvement of personal potential as of articulating the vision for the organization.

The baby bust generation that followed the baby boomers tends to be even more independent and demanding in expectations of managers. To earn their respect and loyalty is an even more arduous task. We see the need to balance style as essential. Genuine, consistently clear, strong, empathic leadership is appealing to all ages.

During the industrial age, America was a primarily manufacturing and agricultural country. Making products and measuring work was more finite than the information age. We are now primarily a country producing information, ideas, and service. We are selling products that are harder to measure. It is increasingly complex to identify poor work performance. Not only is it more difficult to measure what employees really do, but the manager has to prepare for possible lawsuit if steps are taken to dismiss an employee for poor performance. Never before has there been such a need for a manager to be an astute reader of people. Not only must you read it accurately, but you must be able to document the actual behavior. Just documenting your impression is inadequate.

One of the biggest problems facing American management is the unwillingness to confront problem behavior. We tend to promote, transfer, reorganize around, and cater to problem employees. Where is the ability to step up to the problem of confronting the way employees behave while they do their jobs? Is it no longer within the realm of the manager's ability to influence the company culture? We predict that today and tomorrow's manager must be excellent at reading behavior, interpreting it, rewarding and disciplining it. It will no longer be good enough to be a good manager of paper. Managing people is far more complex than just assigning them work.

Knowing your own style is a foundation for increasing your ability to read others. When you begin to take full responsibility for your behavior preferences, behavior begins to get your attention. You learn to recognize the expression of preferences. As you become more aware, you can then make more conscious decisions. Until you are consciously aware that you have choices, you don't exercise them purposefully. Taking responsibility for the strengths and weaknesses of your natural preferences enables you to develop your potential. As you take responsibility for your own behavior, you will find your ability to recognize behavior in others vastly improved. At that point you can make a commitment to improve your people skills and begin immediately *doing* something about it.

A commander of a military installation told me about his recognition of his own style. He scored as an ISTJ ten years ago. As he looked at his very strong patterns and assessed the changes around him, he began a plan of personal development. If you were talking to him today, you would be unaware of his natural ISTJ preferences. He consciously developed his ENFP skills. He talked about how his job required him to stretch across the whole spectrum of preferences. He made a conscious choice to develop his potential, and he developed the skills to do it.

The colonel shared an example of the changing demands. He recalled eighteen years earlier when he had to discipline soldiers: "The punishment that brought the quickest compliance was to mess with their pay or their rank. Today, the only thing that gets their attention is to restrict their freedom. To be assigned to quarters for a weekend definitely hits the hot button. You can restrict their wages but not their freedom without hitting their alert button."

The colonel talked about his natural resistance to change and his respect for hierarchy. If he had not taken responsibility for his preference, he could not have recognized the changing patterns in time to adjust his style. His ability to lead rests clearly on his ability to be a whole person in his expression and decision. Change is inevitable; so why not use it to maximize development?

The information age brings change. Naisbitt and Aburdene in their book *Re-Inventing the Corporation* suggest ten guidelines for looking at the changing requirements. (pp. 45–46)

1. The best and brightest people will gravitate toward those corporations that foster personal growth.
2. The manager's new role is that of coach, teacher, and mentor.
3. The best people want ownership — psychic and literal — in a company; the best companies are providing it.

4. Companies will increasingly turn to third-party contractors, shifting from hired labor to contract labor.
5. Authoritarian management is yielding to a networking people-style of management.
6. Entrepreneurship within the corporations — intrapreneurship — is creating new products and new markets and revitalizing companies inside out.
7. Quality will be paramount.
8. Intuition and creativity are challenging the business-school philosophy of "it's all in the numbers."
9. Large corporations are emulating the positive and productive qualities of small business.
10. The dawn of the information economy has fostered a massive shift from infrastructure to quality of life.

When you review those ten guidelines and recall the need for extroverted interaction with people and introverted depth of understanding, intrapersonal balance is essential. The change and uncertainty is increasing the demand for sensor attention to numbers and details coupled with intuitive insight and innovation. Quality of life demands the blend of both thinker and feeler judgment. Rational thinking coupled with warm and empathic concern for people is essential to sharing ownership with people. People are resisting the authoritarian style of management in their demands for a more people-conscious style of management. Balance of personal style is a viable strategy.

When *In Search of Excellence* burst upon the management scene, people absorbed the term and "excellence" became the buzzword. The search was on to identify excellence as it was seen in the "best-run companies." That search helped us articulate a strong American drive — to be the best. Peters and Waterman identified seven variables to consider in organizing: "structure, strategy, people, management style, systems and procedures, guiding concepts and shared values (i.e., culture), and the present and hoped-for corporate strengths or skills." (p. 10)

In the book *A Passion for Excellence* the focus was on the leadership difference. Eight basics of managerial success were identified: (1) pride in one's own organization; (2) enthusiasm for organization's work; (3) naive customer listening; (4) customer perception of the quality of service of product; (5) employee corporate entrepreneurship; (6) internal corporate entrepreneurship; (7) championing; and (8) trust and vision. (Tom Peters and Nancy Austin)

After thousands of dollars have been spent pursuing excellence, we are still faced with the overwhelming challenge of *being* excellent. We cannot escape the fact that excellence begins with individuals. Excellent internal development of both natural preferences and learned skills is a viable way to be excellent.

Tom Peters's book *Thriving on Chaos* opens with the sentence "There are no excellent companies." Thus, after searching for the golden answer, we are faced with the real challenge of personal growth and development.

A magazine article headline entitled "The 21st Century Executive" indicates our interest in and need for developing leadership. Four roles are identified for tomorrow's boss: global strategist, master of technology, politician par excellence, and leader/motivator. Of the fourth role of leader/motivator their synoposis reads: "Old time charisma is nice, but execs must coach teams as well as command them." (*U.S. News & World Report*, March 7, 1988)

In this search for leadership, Blake and Mouton's managerial grid has been taught for the past twenty years. In their book *Executive Achievement* they state:

> Strong, effective leadership arouses a high degree of involvement and shared commitment among those who work with and through one another. (p. 10)
>
> Effective leadership means finding sound solutions to problems and engaging in innovative activities that are productive, creative, and pertinent to the organization purpose. It conveys the notion that such leadership is being exercised in ways that develop people and that minimize the expense of doing business. For leadership to be truly effective, it has to solve current problems without creating additional ones. (p. 14)

Search current management literature and you see the theme emerging about leadership and development of people. We submit that those who would be in the position of leading people development must first develop themselves. One viable way to do that is to begin with your personal profile and begin to develop balancing skills.

The need for leadership is serious. In John P. Kotter's *The Leadership Factor* he describes the changing demands:

All this activity is forcing firms nearly everywhere to reconsider traditional strategies, policies, and routine methods of doing business. As a result, thousands and thousands of managers and executives are being asked to develop new products, new distribution channels, new marketing methods, new manufacturing processes, new financing strategies, and much more . . . Figuring out the right thing to do in an environment of uncertainty caused by intense competitive activity, and then getting others, often many others, to accept a new way of doing things demands skills and approaches that most managers simply did not need in the relatively calm 1950s, 1960s, and early 1970s. It demands something more than technical expertise, administrative ability, and traditional (especially bureaucratic) management. Operating in the new environment also requires leadership. (p. 9)

LEADERS LEAD THE CHANGE

I have heard no one pose the argument against the need for leadership. We appear to have consensus on the need for it but diversion on how we develop it. Multiple paths lead to leadership development. We are sharing with you one personal development approach that we know works for those willing to commit to the arduous task of personal development.

We have asserted that long-term leadership is the appropriate goal. Many people are capable of short bursts of clarity and focus, but it is a lifetime commitment to personal growth and development that keeps the leader renewed.

Charles Garfield identifies values as the way to excel. In his book *Peak Performers* certain values form a basis for the move toward excelling. The values that underlie peak performers' actions are:

Values achievement and finds his or her primary motivation through mission.

Values contribution, and thus seeks results in real time, and assists in the development of others.

Values self-development, and pursues self-management through self-mastery.

Values creativity, and produces innovation through risk-taking.

Values synergy, and looks for points of alignment among organizational, team, and personal objectives.

Values quality, and pays conscious attention to feedback and course correction.

Values opportunity, and meets the challenge of change. (p. 266)

As we review the multiple routes to leadership development, we return to our original premise: leadership requires people savvy. When you review the ideas of major writers in management, the theme of people development runs consistently throughout.

Our work reinforces the belief that organizations cannot be run by committee. Time rarely allows everyone's participation in a decision. Someone has to call the shot. There are times for consensus and times for command. The wise leader knows when to use consensus, when to use motivation, and when to use command.

You know when you are in the presence of a leader. Something happens. The leader affects you. Let me try to describe what I feel in the presence of a man who meets the criteria for leadership.

I find myself standing taller, thinking more clearly, seeing things freshly, considering greater risk, and performing in ways I didn't know I could. I realize potential that I had not even recognized was in me. I expand my thinking, increase my production, confront my fear of failing, and gain incredible insights.

As I have come to trust his wisdom, I find increasing willingness to risk developing my potential.

Leaders don't coddle people. They demand self-discipline, quality contribution, personal responsibility, and mature responses. In short, they hold us responsible for our actions.

Leaders recognize our natural patterns but don't allow us to hide behind them. They inspire, threaten, lead, encourage, and guide our development.

The more balanced the development on the Myers-Briggs dichotomous dimensions, the harder to categorize the style. At the point where you have balanced type development, you utilize all eight possibilities . . . You use thinker and feeler judgment, sensor and intuitor perception, and match extroversion-introversion to situational need.

Extroverted leaders would maximize their propensity for action, people, and external events. They would develop their introverted skills of concentration, depth, and introspection. Introverts would do just the reverse. To be comfortable in the outer world of interaction and also in the inner world of introspection, you must systematically access the power of both.

Sensors would maximize their preference for sensory verification of the reality of their external world. They would add intuitive skills to their normal preference for sensibility and realism. They would develop the skill of synthesizing random information to discover patterns and implications. They would develop innovative ways of seeing and assessing. Intuitors would develop their skills for seeing details as they currently exist in the external environment. Repeatedly, in both the case studies and the review of management literature, we have seen the need for fresh thinking and realistic action.

Thinkers would maximize their preference for logical analysis, justice, and objectivity. They would develop feeler skills in interpreting subjective values and personal attractions. Thinkers would develop the skills to accept feelings as "real" data and would no longer feel the need to deny or rearrange feelings. Thinkers would include feeler data into their rationale, knowing that antiseptic, objective solutions may fail because people won't buy them — they don't feel good about them. Likewise, feelers would maximize their preference for the people perspective and develop their analytical skills. Development of both the objective and subjective viewpoints should give a clearer perspective. The head may be impressive, but it is the heart that motivates.

Judge-controllers would maximize their preference for order, planning, and control while developing their perceiver skills of adaptability, flexibility, and spontaneity. Perceivers would work on their natural skills and develop decisiveness, preparedness, and task closure.

We can read about leadership, talk about excellence, and dream about people development. At some point, we have to actually do something. Actions are what count.

Personal development is difficult. It is painful at times; it is inspiring at times; and it always includes risk. Leadership is not for the weak, the lazy, the arrogant, the dominator, or the con artist. Long-term leadership requires courage, commitment, sacrifice, and service.

Those people who would tell you that leadership means privilege of position and power to get what you want aren't talking about the kind of leadership we are suggesting. Leadership means the privilege of service. Only those who are truly mature enough to understand that power increases as you empower others will see leadership as service.

A balanced style provides a foundation for long-term leadership. The leader knows that full potential is never realized; thus, the need for the leader's ongoing, brutal examination of motives and actions together with continual development of potential is a challenge that continues as long as breath is in the body. Leadership requires growth and development all the days that we live.

Abuse of power has in the past been mistaken for leadership. To commit yourself to the painful task of confrontation of fears and weaknesses is opposite the cultural norms of ease and pleasure. Developing leadership demands risk-taking, courage, and unyielding determination. Truly, THE LEADER IS

more fearless . . . for fears have already been confronted . . . they are old familiar foes of the warrior . . .

more clear . . . for perception has been broadened to see both near and far, to see detail and implication, to see the vision and the plan for achieving it, to see behavior and the motive driving it . . .

more unlimited . . . for potential is continually being turned into action, use of power is continually self-monitored, total commitment to the vision produces power and authority, and confrontation of problems is a way of life . . .

more wise . . . for both power and powerlessness forged the character, both success and failure provided the compassion, and both pain and satisfaction strengthened the foundation . . . and both natural preferences and learned skills provide the balance . . .

and *more courageous* . . . for the shattering pain of self-confrontation tears away illusion of self-importance, arrogance, and defensiveness, and leaves the truth of our existence . . . and what could be stronger than that?

The leadership equation involves balancing style for leadership enhancement. Good luck!

References

Bennis, Warren, and Burt Nanus. *Leaders: The Strategies for Taking Charge.* New York: Harper & Row, 1985.

Blake, Robert R., and Jane S. Mouton. *Executive Achievement: Making It at the Top.* New York: McGraw-Hill Book Company, 1986.

Corbin, Carolyn. *Strategies 2000.* Austin: Eakin Press, 1986.

Dean, Douglas, John Mihalasky, Sheila Ostrander, and Lynn Schroeder. *Executive ESP.* Englewood Cliffs, NJ: Prentice-Hall Inc., 1976.

Garfield, Charles. *Peak Performers: The New Heroes of American Business.* New York: Avon, 1986.

Jung, C. G., revised by R. F. C. Hull of the translation by H. G. Baynes. *Psychological Types.* Princeton University Press, 1976.

Keirsey, David, and Marilyn Bates. *Please Understand Me: Character and Temperament Types.* Del Mar, CA: Prometheus Nemesis Books, 1978.

Kotter, John P. *The Leadership Factor.* New York: The Free Press, 1988.

Myers, Isabel Briggs, and Mary H. McCaulley. *Manual: A Guide to the Development and Use of the Myers-Briggs Type Indicator.* Palo Alto, CA: Consulting Psychologists Press, 1985.

Naisbitt, John, and Patricia Aburdene. *Re-Inventing the Corporation.* New York: Warner Books, 1985.

Peters, Tom. *Thriving on Chaos.* New York: Alfred A. Knopf, 1987.

———, and Nancy Austin. *A Passion for Excellence: The Leadership Difference.* New York: Random House, 1985.

Peters, Thomas J., and Robert H. Waterman, Jr. *In Search of Excellence: Lessons from America's Best-Run Companies.* New York: Harper & Row, 1982.

Rowan, Roy. *The Intuitive Manager.* New York: Berkley Books, 1986.

Work, Clemens P., with Beth Brophy, Andrea Gabor, Robert F. Black, Mike Tharp, and Alice Z. Cuneo. "The 21st Century Executive," *U.S. News & World Report* (March 7, 1988), 48–51.